Headway

Academic Skills
Reading, Writing, and Study Skills
LEVEL 2 **Student's Book**

Sarah Philpot
Series Editors: Liz and John Soars

D1350658

OXFORD

CONTENTS

1 International student

READING SKILLS Following instructions • Reading methods
WRITING SKILLS Checking your writing • Writing an informal email
VOCABULARY DEVELOPMENT A dictionary entry • Recording vocabulary (1)

READING Going abroad to study

1 Personal information often appears on documents, especially official documents. Use the ideas in the box to say what personal information is on … ?

- a birth certificate
- a driving licence
- a bank statement
- an exam certificate

name	date of birth	address	parents' names
grades	driver number	account number	
name of school or university	place of birth		

2 Simon Elliot lives in Geneva, Switzerland. He is returning to the UK to study. Answer the questions.

1 Label the documents. Which is … ?

- a passport
- an informal letter
- a formal letter
- an application form

2 Where is Simon going?
3 What is he going to study?
4 Who is John?

---

a

University of
WEST LONDON

Apartment 25,
Lac de Leman Building,
Geneva,
Switzerland

Dear Mr Elliot,

We have pleasure in offering you a place at the University of West London to study for a Master's degree (MSc) in Applied Biochemistry. The academic year commences on 10 October and classes start …

---

c

Apartment 25,
Lac de Leman Building,
Geneva,
Switzerland

email simon.elliot@gen.com

Dear John,

Just writing to let you know that I've got a place at West London University to do my MSc! So, I'm finally coming back to London. I'm really looking forward to seeing you again. I'm not sure where I'll be living. I'm applying for accommodation with a host family – that way I won't have to cook! I just hope that there's a vegetarian family available. As soon as I know my new address, I'll email or ring you, and we can meet! Do you like the photos I've sent? Do you remember …

---

d

United Kingdom of Great Britain and Northern Ireland

Passport

Passport No
012234556

Surname
ELLIOT

Given names
SIMON

Nationality
BRITISH CITIZEN

Date of birth
22 OCTOBER 1989

Date of issue
06 JUNE 2010

Date of expiry
05 JUNE 2020

3 Look at the application form. What is it for?

4 Read the documents on page 4. Use the information to complete the application form for Simon.

Read STUDY SKILL

b

University of
WEST LONDON

Please print.
Use black or blue ink only.
Tick (✓) the relevant boxes.

Application for Accommodation

Family name ____Elliot_____

First name(s) _____

Male/Female (Delete as appropriate)   **Single** ☐ **Married** ☐

Children   Yes ☐   No ☐   Number ☐

Date of birth [/ /]   **Nationality** _____

Passport/ID number _____

Home address _____

Postcode _____   Country _____

Course title _____

Course start date [/ /]

Type of accommodation
☐ Host family
☐ University hall of residence
☐ Shared house

Special diet   Yes ☐   No ☐
Please specify:
_____
_____
_____
_____

How and why do you read?

5 What do *you* read? Tick (✓) the different reading materials a–j that you read.

a ☐ textbooks   f ☐ reports
b ☐ novels   g ☐ timetables
c ☐ emails   h ☐ indexes
d ☐ search engine finds i ☐ a dictionary
e ☐ journals   j ☐ instruction manuals

6 Which reading materials from exercise 5 do you read for pleasure; for work; for your studies? Make three lists.

7 Read the handout for new students about reading. Answer the questions.
1 Which two ways of reading are the quickest?
2 Which way would you read for enjoyment?
3 Which way of reading is the slowest?

Effective Reading

During your course, you will do a lot of reading. It is essential that you learn how to be an effective and efficient reader in order to make the best of your study time. Learning to be a good reader takes practice. You need to develop different strategies or methods of reading.

Skimming

Sometimes you will read just to get a general idea of a text. This is skim reading. First, identify your reason for reading, for example, to decide whether an article meets your needs, or perhaps to understand a writer's attitude. To do this, read the text very quickly. Don't worry about reading and understanding everything. Instead, look particularly at the first and last paragraphs, and the first and last sentences of paragraphs. These often summarize the main points.

Scanning

Sometimes you will read quickly to find particular pieces of information, for example, a statistic, a date, a person's name, or the name of a place. Again, you do not need to read every word to find this information. Instead, scan the text using a finger or a pencil to move quickly through the words. You could time yourself to see how long it takes you to find the information. Always try to improve your speed.

Intensive reading

Sometimes you read for every detail, for example, a description of a process, the results of a scientific study, or a set literature text. To do this, take your time. Stop and think about what you are reading. Have you understood the text? You may need to read the text more than once, in order to make notes or highlight important points for future reference. This is called intensive reading or study reading.

Extensive reading

Sometimes you will read for pleasure – perhaps as extra research, or purely for interest. You may concentrate, but you don't have to worry about detail. This is extensive reading.

We do not always read the same kinds of texts in the same way, and we often use more than one method of reading for a single text. Your reason for reading will help you decide how to read.

University of
WEST LONDON

CJ Study Skills ER07

8 Choose five examples of reading materials from exercise 5 on page 5. *Why* and *how* do you read?

text book	Why?	to find a relevant chapter
		to take notes
	How?	scan contents page
		read intensively

9 Look back at exercises 2 and 4 on pages 4 and 5. In which exercise did you 'skim' and in which did you 'scan'?

WRITING A host family

1 Imagine you are going abroad to do a short course and are going to live with a host family. What information would you give them and what information would you want? Think about:

dates	food	personal information	transport	computer access	hobbies

2 Burcu Sancak, a Turkish student, is writing to her host family. Read her email. Tick (✓) the items from exercise 1 that she mentions.

Accommodation message

From: Burcu Sancak [bsancak@mailnet.com.tr] **Sent:** 16 July 2011
To: Mr and Mrs Baker
Subject: **Accommodation**

Dear Mr and Mrs Baker,

I'm very happy to accept your offer of accomodation. I'm really excited about coming to London for the first time to do an English course.

I am in my last year of school and next year I want to go to university to study english Language and Literature. at the moment i am preparing for my final exams, so I'm working very hard. When I'm not so bisy, I spend a lot of time reading, but I also enjoy sports I play basketball for my school team once a week. I also enjoy swiming. Is there a sports club with a swimming pool near your house.

As I mentioned in my last email, my course starts on 24th July but I'm coming two days earlier and my plain arrives at heathrow on the 22nd at 14.25 Could you tell me the best way of getting from the airport to your house?

I hope to here from you soon and I'm really looking forward to seeing you in London.

Best wishes,

Burcu Sancak

3 **Read STUDY SKILL** Read Burcu's email again. There are 12 mistakes (capital letters, full stops, question marks, and spelling). Find and correct them.

STUDY SKILL Checking your writing

Every time you write, remember to check your work for:

- capital letters at the beginning of sentences and for proper nouns (names of people, cities, and countries)
- full stops at the end of sentences
- question marks at the end of questions
- spelling mistakes. Use a dictionary or computer spellchecker to check your spelling. Keep a record of any words you misspell. Learn the correct spelling.

Writing an informal email

4 Imagine you are going to stay with a family for a short course. Write them an email. Write about 100 words.

- Say you accept their offer of a room.
- Tell them about your studies and your hobbies.
- Give them information about your arrival.
- Ask for information you would like.

Check your work carefully. Give it to another student to check again.

VOCABULARY DEVELOPMENT Dictionary work

1 Put the following words into alphabetical order as quickly as you can. Compare your order with a partner.

> brainstorm skim question accommodation dictionary
> biography student vocabulary writing punctuation scan
> pronunciation computer technology study voice keyboard

2 **Read STUDY SKILL** Here is an entry from the *Oxford Student's Dictionary*. Label the parts of the entry 1–5 using the words in the box.

> part of speech definition pronunciation
> example sentence stress mark

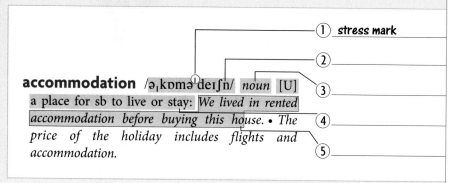

STUDY SKILL A dictionary entry

Choose an English–English dictionary and make sure it is a recent edition.

Dictionaries include a lot of useful information.

For example:

- parts of speech
- stress
- pronunciation
- definitions
- example sentences

Be careful! Some words have more than one meaning and use. Make sure you look at the correct part of a definition.

3 Look at the word card. What five pieces of information does it give you about the word *study*?

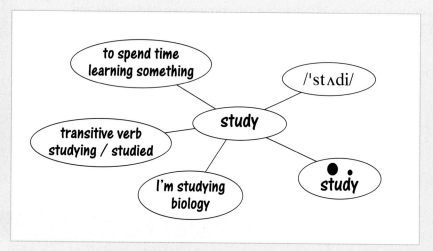

4 Make word cards for the underlined words in 1–6. Use your dictionary. **Read STUDY SKILL**

1 I am studying <u>Chemical</u> Engineering.
2 We <u>scan</u> a timetable to get the information we want.
3 Correct <u>punctuation</u> is very important in good writing.
4 Always check in a <u>dictionary</u> if you are not sure about how a word is spelt.
5 A <u>biography</u> is the story of someone's life.
6 Novels, plays, and poetry are examples of <u>literature</u>.

STUDY SKILL Recording vocabulary (1)

It is important to keep a record of new vocabulary. You may wish to keep these records in a vocabulary notebook or in a special vocabulary file on the computer.

Wherever you record new vocabulary, it is helpful to note more than the translation. Also note, for example:

- the pronunciation
- the stressed syllables
- part of speech
- associated words and grammar, e.g. a *biography of someone*

REVIEW

1 Complete the visa application form about you.

VISA APPLICATION

Please print. Use black or blue ink only. Tick (✓) relevant boxes.

Family name _____   **First name** _____

                                                              Middle name(s) _____

Date of birth _____

Place of birth _____

Nationality _____   **Passport/ID number** _____

                                                              Place of issue _____

Sex Male ☐ Female ☐

Marital status _____

Title Dr ☐ Mr ☐ Mrs ☐ Ms ☐ Miss ☐ Other (specify) _____

Home address _____   **Email address** _____

                                _____   **Home or mobile telephone number**

                                  _____   _____

                                  _____

Reasons for visit

  Business ☐

  Study ☐

  Tourism ☐

  Family visit ☐

Other (specify) _____

Duration of visit

  1–7 days ☐

  8–15 days ☐

  Up to one month ☐

  More than one month (specify length) _____

Date of arrival (if known) _____   **Date of departure (if known)** _____

Address in country (if known) _____

_____

---

2 Use your dictionary to correct the spelling of the underlined words.

  1 She <u>payed</u> for her books with a credit card.

  2 He <u>bougth</u> a new car last month.

  3 What subject are you <u>studing</u>?

  4 My parents always give me good <u>advise</u>.

  5 Have you <u>applyed</u> to university yet?

  6 Please put the books back on the correct <u>shelfs</u>.

3 Review the texts and vocabulary in Unit 1. Choose at least five words that are new for you. Make word cards for them.

2 Where in the world ...?

READING SKILLS Skimming and scanning
WRITING SKILLS Brainstorming ideas • Linking ideas (1) • Writing a description of my country
VOCABULARY DEVELOPMENT Synonyms and antonyms • Recording vocabulary (2)

READING Three countries

1 Look at photos a–c and skim texts 1–3 on page 11. Match them with the titles below. **Read STUDY SKILL**

☐ ☐ Cities, Deserts, Seas

☐ ☐ A World on an Island

☐ ☐ Your Dream Castle?

> **STUDY SKILL** Skimming and scanning
>
> Remember there are two ways of reading quickly:
> - skimming for the general idea
> - scanning for particular information

2 Scan the texts. Find information to complete the table.

	location	important date	economy	attractions	language(s)
Singapore			strong economy, tourism		Malay, English, Mandarin, Tamil
Morocco	North Africa			Fez, beaches, Sahara Desert	
Wales					

3 Scan the texts again to answer the questions.

Which country ...

- has a border with England?
- has a desert?
- has a lot of ancient castles?
- is an island?
- has man-made beaches?
- is ruled by a king?
- has a wild coastline?
- is in South-East Asia?
- has an ocean to the west, and a sea to the north?

4 Scan the texts to match a word in A with a word in B, and a definition in C.

A	B	C
historic	1 _____ beaches	a ☐ beaches made by people, not by nature
natural	2 _____ city	b ☐ coal, gas, oil, and fresh water are all examples of these
tourist	3 _____ destination	c ☐ a popular place to go on holiday
national	4 _____ language	d ☐ a place with a long and important history
man-made	5 _____ resources	e ☐ the main language used in a country
official	6 _____ assembly	f ☐ the group of people chosen to govern a country

5 Read the texts again more slowly. In pairs, discuss similarities and differences between the three countries and your own country.

1

The Republic of Singapore is an island in South-East Asia, just 137km north of the Equator. It became an independent city-state in 1965. Singapore has few natural resources. However, it developed a strong economy and is a popular tourist destination. People come here for its fabulous shopping, the famous Singapore Zoo, and its beautiful man-made beaches. Singapore has a rich mixture of people and many languages are spoken here, including Malay, English, Mandarin, and Tamil.

2

The Kingdom of Morocco is a country in North Africa. It has the Atlantic Ocean to the west, the Mediterranean Sea to the north, Algeria to the east, and Western Sahara to the south. It became an independent kingdom in 1956. Its economy depends on mining and tourism. Morocco's attractions include the historic city of Fez, the wonderful beaches on the Atlantic and Mediterranean, and the Sahara Desert. Arabic is the official language, although French is often used for business.

3

Wales is in northern Europe. It is part of the United Kingdom. It borders England to the east, and has the Irish Sea on the west. Wales was ruled by England for many centuries, but in 1999 its own National Assembly was created. Farming and tourism are important parts of its economy. Tourists come to Wales to see its many ancient castles, to walk and climb in its beautiful mountains, or to walk along its wild coastline. Although most people speak English, both Welsh and English are the official languages.

WRITING My country

1 Complete the diagram about France using the topic areas and examples in the box. **Read STUDY SKILL**

skiing in the Alps	economy	coal
the Atlantic Ocean	Spain	1789
tourism	French	Euro Disney

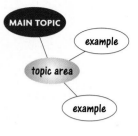
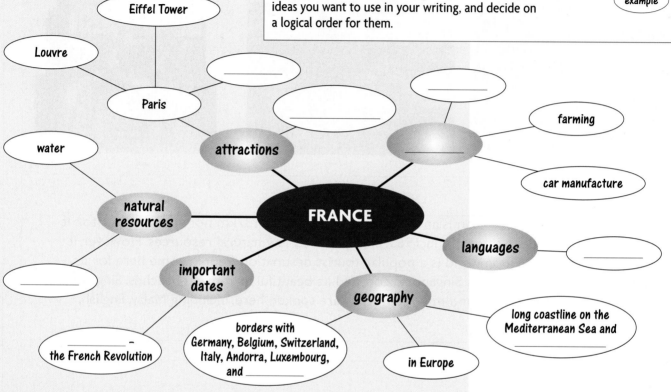

2 Complete the paragraph about France. Use information from the diagram in exercise 1.

FRANCE – SOMETHING FOR EVERYONE!

France is a large country in ¹_____ . It has ²_____ with many countries, including Germany, Italy, and Spain. It was ruled by a king. However, after the revolution in ³_____ , it became a republic. France has good natural resources, such as water and ⁴_____ . Farming, car manufacturing, and ⁵_____ are other important parts of its economy. The capital of France is Paris, which lies on the River Seine. Many tourists stay in the city to see the ⁶_____ Tower, or to visit the world-famous Louvre Museum and the many other attractions. There are also lots of other things to do outside Paris. You can go skiing in the ⁷_____ , visit ⁸_____ , or go swimming in the Mediterranean. Although the official language is French, many people speak a little English. So, whatever your interests and wherever you come from, France has something for you.

3 Look back at the text on page 12. Write the topic areas from the box next to numbers 1–5 in the order they appear in the text.

languages	attractions	geography	important date(s)	economy

1 _____ 2 _____ 3 _____ 4 _____ 5 _____

4 With a partner, quickly brainstorm ideas about your country. Write your ideas on a diagram. Use the topic areas from exercise 3.

5 **Read STUDY SKILL** Underline other examples of *but*, *however*, and *although* in the three texts on page 11.

> ### STUDY SKILL Linking ideas (1)
>
> Linking ideas in a clear and logical way is part of good writing. Use *but*, *however*, and *although* to contrast two ideas.
>
> Look at sentences **a** and **b**. Compare the way *but*, *however*, and *although* are used to link them. What differences are there?
>
> **a** *The official language is French.*
> **b** *Many people speak a little English.*
>
> *The official language is French, **but** many people speak a little English.*
> *The official language is French. **However**, many people speak a little English.*
> ***Although** the official language is French, many people speak a little English.*
> *The official language is French, **although** many people speak a little English.*

6 Link the pairs of sentences using the word in brackets.

1 Many people think that Sydney is the capital of Australia. Canberra is really the capital. (but)

_____

2 The Amazon is the longest river in South America. The Nile is the longest river in the world. (however)

_____

3 Mount Everest is the highest mountain in the world. It is not the most difficult to climb. (although)

_____

4 It is very hot in the Sahara during the day. It can be very cold at night. (although)

_____

Writing a description of my country

7 Write a paragraph of about 150 words describing your country. Use your ideas from exercise 4. Link them using *but*, *however*, and *although*.

VOCABULARY DEVELOPMENT Organizing vocabulary (1)

1 Put the words in the box into two groups. Then organize them in order of size (**smallest ⟵⟶ biggest**) or speed (**slowest ⟵⟶ fastest**).

bicycle   sea   ocean   aeroplane   space rocket   lake   car   pond

2 **Read STUDY SKILL** Match 1–5 with synonyms (=) and antonyms(≠) from the box.

Read STUDY SKILL

frontier   big   new   noisy   old   quiet   small   seashore

1 border   = _____
2 coastline   = _____
3 modern   = _____
            ≠ _____
4 large   = _____
            ≠ _____
5 loud   = _____
            ≠ _____

> **STUDY SKILL** Synonyms and antonyms
>
> A **synonym** is a word or phrase that has the same meaning as another word or phrase.
>
> An **antonym** is a word or a phrase that means the opposite of another word or phrase.

3 Use the words in the box to label the compass.

north   south   east   west   north-west   south-west   north-east   south-east

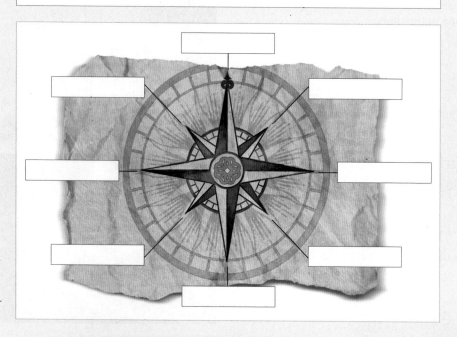

4 Look at the words in the box. Organize them into four groups of four words each. Record them using different methods. **Read STUDY SKILL**

a cottage   clean   the North Pole   deserts   dirty
the Earth   lakes   mountains   a house   unpolluted
an apartment block   polluted   a skyscraper
rainforests   the South Pole   the Equator

> **STUDY SKILL** Recording vocabulary (2)
>
> Recording words in groups can make them easier to remember. You can use:
> - diagrams like the ones in this unit
> - a scale as in exercise 1
> - synonyms and antonyms as in exercise 2
> - a picture with labels as in exercise 3
>
> Continue to add new words to each group as you learn them.

REVIEW

1 Go back through Unit 2. Add examples to the table. Write the definite article *the* where necessary.

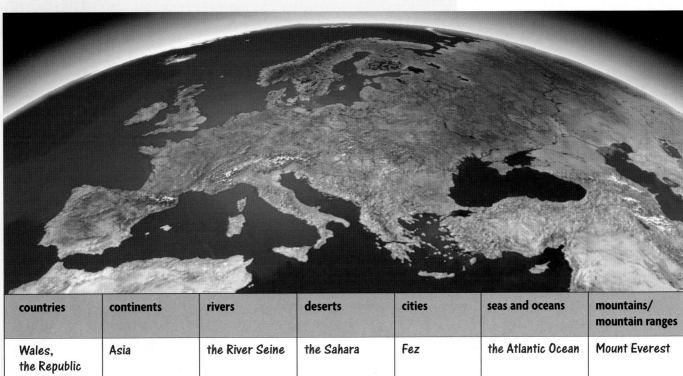

countries	continents	rivers	deserts	cities	seas and oceans	mountains/ mountain ranges
Wales, the Republic of Singapore	Asia	the River Seine	the Sahara	Fez	the Atlantic Ocean	Mount Everest

2 When is the definite article *the* used? Complete the rules.

> **RULES**
>
> Use *the* with rivers, deserts, mountain ranges, _____ and oceans.
> Do not use *the* with most countries, _____ , mountains, and _____ .

3 Add some examples from your own country or region to the table.

4 Make sentences 1–8 true by replacing the word in *italics* with another word from Unit 2.

1 Asia is a large *country*.
2 Morocco has beaches on the Atlantic *Sea*.
3 Spain is *north* of France.
4 A *castle* is where you can go to see lots of different animals.
5 *A lake* is bigger than a sea.
6 Sydney is a very *old* city.
7 Russia is a *small* country.
8 A village is *bigger* than a town.

5 Make your own records of any new words. Use the methods from this unit.

3 Newspaper articles

READING SKILLS Predicting content • Meaning from context
WRITING SKILLS Sentences • Paragraphs • Varying the structure • Writing an article
VOCABULARY DEVELOPMENT Antonyms from prefixes

READING An unexpected journey

1 Look at the headline and pictures in the newspaper article. What do you think the story is about? Discuss your ideas with a partner.

A free flight to Dubai

A twenty-three-year-old Dutch student has enjoyed a short but unexpected holiday in Dubai. Mr Frank Vreede, a business student, had taken a part-time job at Schiphol Airport to help pay for his studies. He worked as a **baggage handler** and was responsible for loading the suitcases into the **hold** of passenger planes.

Last Friday night, after an exhausting day in the university library preparing for his final exams, Frank was loading a plane at the airport. He was waiting for the next baggage truck to arrive and he felt tired. He decided to have a quick rest, so he sat down in the hold of the plane and shut his eyes – just for a moment.

However, while he was sleeping, the plane **took off**. An hour later, Frank woke up and was **horrified** to discover that the plane was in the air. There was a terrible noise from the engines, and he tried not to panic. It was dark, uncomfortable and very, very cold. Frank knew the flight would be long because it was an airline from the Middle East. He also knew he could not survive the freezing temperatures. It was an impossible situation.

He decided to make as much noise as possible. He **banged** on the ceiling of the baggage hold and shouted at the top of his voice. Luckily, a passenger heard the noise and called a flight attendant, who immediately informed the pilot. Once the captain understood what was happening, he ordered hot air to be pumped into the hold.

When the plane arrived at Dubai International Airport, an ambulance was waiting to take a very cold and frightened Mr Vreede to hospital. Doctors examined him, but he was **unhurt** and was allowed to leave after a few hours. News spread quickly about this 'stowaway'. The Managing Director of one of Dubai's top hotels offered him a free room for the weekend. 'He must have wanted to come to Dubai very much if he was prepared to travel in the hold!' joked the MD.

'Everyone's been so kind,' said Mr Vreede. 'I'm really enjoying my stay in Dubai and I'm getting a lot of rest, so I won't fall asleep on the job again!'

When Frank returned to Schiphol Airport on Monday, his friends and **relatives** were overjoyed to see him. 'When he didn't come home after his evening **shift** on Friday, I called the airport – but nobody had seen him for hours,' his mother said to reporters. Frank explained that he was very lucky because it is possible to die of cold in the hold of an aircraft. He **apologized** to his boss for sleeping at work instead of working, and promised it would not happen again. 'During the flight I was **petrified**. I thought I was going to die!' said Mr Vreede. 'I wouldn't want to do it again. Next time, I'll catch a regular flight!'

2 **Read STUDY SKILL** Make questions about the article. Use the question words in the box.

| Why …?   Where …?   Who …?   When …?   What …?   How …? |

Why was it a free flight?

STUDY SKILL Predicting content

Predicting the content of a text prepares you for what you are about to read. Being well-prepared helps comprehension.

Before you read a text:

■ look at the title   ■ look at any pictures

Use these to get an idea of what the text is about. Ask some questions (*Who? Where? Why?* etc.) to help you predict the content and to focus on the information you need.

---

3 Skim the text to get a general idea of the story. Were your ideas right? Does the text answer your questions?

4 Read the article more slowly and answer the questions.

1 **Who** is the article about?
2 **What** other people are mentioned in the article?
3 **Where** did the events happen?
4 **When** did the events happen?
5 **What** was the problem?
6 **How** was the problem solved?

Compare your answers with a partner.

5 **Read STUDY SKILL** Copy the table. Guess the meaning of the words in bold in the article *A Free Flight to Dubai*. Use the part of speech and the context to help.

STUDY SKILL Meaning from context

Texts often contain words we don't know. Looking up every word takes time and slows down your reading.

To help you guess the meaning from the context:

■ look at the words and sentences around the unknown word.
■ identify the part of speech.
■ use your knowledge of the world (what you already know about the situation).
■ think about whether the word has a generally negative or positive meaning.
■ replace the unknown word with another word with a similar meaning and check that it makes sense in the sentence.

---

word	part of speech	context	guess
baggage handler	noun	job or duty / airport responsible for loading suitcases/ passenger planes	person who puts bags on a plane

6 Compare your guesses with a partner. Check meanings in a dictionary.

7 Underline other new words in the article. Make guesses about them. Check your guesses in a dictionary.

WRITING Mistaken identity

1 Look at paragraph 1 of the newspaper article *A Case of Mistaken Identity* on page 19. Separate it into six sentences. Punctuate the sentences correctly.

`Read STUDY SKILL`

> **STUDY SKILL** Sentences
>
> - write short, clear sentences.
> - join ideas and sentences using linking words, for example, *however*, *after*, etc. (see Study Skill p13).
> - punctuate correctly using capital letters, full stops, question marks, and exclamation marks.

2 Complete paragraph 2 of the article using the words in the box.

> after   and   unfortunately   but   because   so

3 Read the beginnings of paragraphs 3 and 4 of the article. Choose which sentences, a or b, from 1–5 belong to each paragraph. Write the paragraphs.

> 1 a Then the car stopped in front of a large conference centre. **Paragraph 3**
>   b He told John that everything was ready for him. **Paragraph 4**
>
> 2 a Mr Taylor jumped out of the car with his briefcase and rushed into the centre. ③
>   b 'Follow me, please,' he said.
>
> 3 a John Taylor got up, checked his tie was straight, and picked up his briefcase.
>   b There, to his relief, he was greeted in English by the conference organizer. ③
>
> 4 a He followed the organizer out of the room.
>   b 'Welcome to Paris, Mr Taylor,' said the smartly-dressed organizer and he led John Taylor down a long corridor and into a small room. ③
>
> 5 a After giving Mr Taylor a coffee, the organizer went off to make sure everything was ready. ③
>   b The organizer opened a door and led John Taylor into a large hall full of … schoolchildren!

4 Look at the next two paragraphs. Which is paragraph 5? Which is paragraph 6? `Read STUDY SKILL`

> **STUDY SKILL** Paragraphs
>
> To help your writing flow:
> - group ideas on the same topic together in a paragraph.
> - make sure there is a clear link between the content of one paragraph and the next.

5 Read paragraph 1 of the article again. Find an example of the Present Perfect, Past Simple, Past Continuous, and Past Perfect. `Read STUDY SKILL`

> **STUDY SKILL** Varying the structure
>
> Interesting writing often contains a variety of tenses.
>
> For example:
> - Past Simple – *It was a comfortable flight.*
> - Past Continuous – *He was loading a plane at the airport.*
> - Present Perfect – *He has been to France before.*
> - Past Perfect – *He had taken a part-time job at the airport.*

Mr Taylor

A case of mistaken identity

1 have you ever been mistaken for someone else last week Mr John Taylor, an Australian businessman, went to Paris for an important meeting he was sent by the Australian government to give a speech to French businessmen and women it was to encourage more trade it was, therefore, a very important speech and Mr Taylor had prepared it carefully at the same time a Mr Paul Taylor was also travelling on the same flight to Paris

2 It was a comfortable flight [1]_____ his plane arrived on time. John Taylor was expecting a driver to pick him up from the airport. [2]_____ going through customs and immigration control, he went to find the driver. He saw a man who was holding a sign saying 'Mr Taylor', [3]_____ he introduced himself. The driver replied in French. [4]_____ , Mr Taylor did not speak French, [5]_____ he did understand the words 'hotel' and 'seminar'. [6]_____ the meeting was early that morning, John Taylor decided to go straight to the seminar. He nodded his head at the driver and repeated 'seminar'.

3 While the car was speeding through Paris, Mr Taylor went through his notes one more time.

4 The organizer returned a few minutes later.

Paragraph 6
This case of mistaken identity was quickly noticed and put right. Both Mr Taylors, Paul and John, were put into taxis and driven at great speed to their correct meetings. Fortunately, both presentations were hugely successful, as they discovered when they were seated next to each other on the flight back to Australia!

Paragraph 5
John Taylor looked around in horror at the children. Then he heard the organizer asking them to welcome Mr Paul Taylor. He was going to tell them about kangaroo farming in Australia! Meanwhile, on the other side of the city, Mr Paul Taylor was also in a large hall full of people. Paul, dressed in blue jeans and cowboy boots, was staring in horror at 200 smartly-suited businessmen and women.

VOCABULARY DEVELOPMENT Word-building (1)

1 Put the adjectives from this unit with the correct prefix in the table. Use a dictionary to help you. `Read STUDY SKILL`

expected	regular	comfortable	possible	hurt	important

un-	unexpected	_____
	_____	_____
in-	_____	_____
	_____	
il-	_____	_____
	_____	
im-	_____	_____
	_____	_____
	_____	
ir-	_____	_____
	_____	

STUDY SKILL Antonyms from prefixes

The antonyms of some words can be made by adding a prefix such as *un-*, *in-*, *im-*, for example, *successful/**un**successful*.

In other cases, the antonym is a completely different word, for example, *good/**bad***.

When you look up a new word in the dictionary, make a note of its antonym.

un-
in-
il- *im-* *ir-*

2 Use a dictionary to identify the correct prefixes for the adjectives in the box. Add them to the table in exercise 1.

appropriate	direct	experienced	patient	relevant	mature
legal	responsible	logical	legible	mobile	personal

3 Look back at the table in exercise 1. Can you see any general rules about when to use *il-*, *im-*, and *ir-*? Complete the rules.

> **RULES** *il-*, *im-*, *ir-*
>
> *il-* is used with words beginning with _____ .
> *im-* is often used with words beginning with _____ and _____ .
> *ir-* is used with words beginning with _____ .

4 Match words 1–7 with antonyms a–g.

1 ☐ different   a low
2 ☐ easy   b maximum
3 ☐ high   c small
4 ☐ large   d public
5 ☐ late   e early
6 ☐ minimum   f difficult / hard
7 ☐ private   g the same

REVIEW

1 Look at the titles of these newspaper articles. What do you think each article is about? Work with a partner and write five questions about each article.

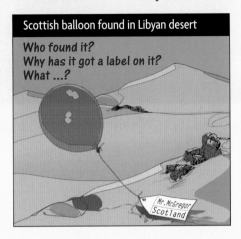

Scottish balloon found in Libyan desert

Who found it?
Why has it got a label on it?
What ...?

The first-class violin

Fly me to the moon – return ticket, please

2 Read the beginning of John Taylor's talk. The words in bold are different parts of speech of the nonsense word **naman**. What part of speech are they? Choose from the box.

> verb x (2)   noun x (3)   adjective x (2)

> Good ¹**naman**, everyone. I am sorry for ²**namaning** late, but thank you for being so patient. As you know, I am here to ³**naman** about the possibilities for increased commerce between our two ⁴**namanies** and I hope that this talk will lead to a fruitful discussion. Our two countries have had very good relations for many ⁵**namanies**, in fact since 1872! Last year, many of our ⁶**namanical** students came here to study your farming systems. It was a very ⁷**namaning** visit and they learnt a lot. In the future, . . .

3 Guess their meaning from the context and replace them with an appropriate real word.

Good ¹**naman**, everyone. = *Good morning/afternoon, everyone.*

4 Make notes about each of the pictures. Write a paragraph of 20–40 words for each one in the past tense. Give your complete article a title.

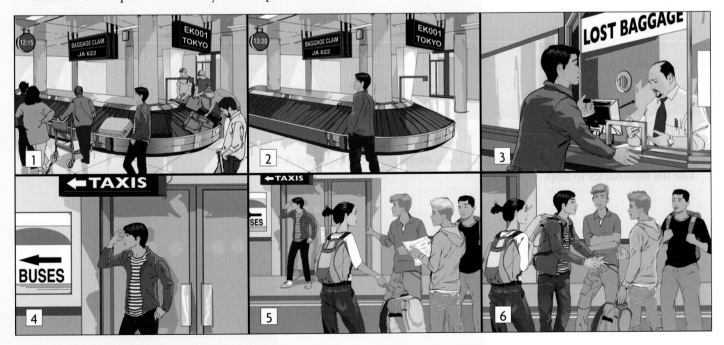

4 Modern technology

READING SKILLS Identifying the main message – topic sentences
WRITING SKILLS Organizing ideas (1) • Linking ideas (2) • Writing a discursive essay
VOCABULARY DEVELOPMENT Avoiding repetition (1)

READING Innovations

1 Skim the articles and letters on page 23. Answer the questions.

1 Where would you expect to find a page like this?
2 How many articles are there?
3 What is the topic of each article?
4 How many letters are there?
5 What piece of technology is each letter about?

2 [Read STUDY SKILL] Scan the text *The Silent Plane* and the readers' letters opposite. Pay attention to topic sentences only. Are the statements true (**T**) or false (**F**)?

1 Maybe one day planes won't make a noise.   *T*
2 Noise is being reduced in two ways.
3 The project to build the plane hasn't begun yet.
4 Mr Campbell is happy with his computer.
5 The writer of the third letter wants help.
6 Paula Adams' opinion is the same as an earlier letter writers.

> ### STUDY SKILL
> #### Identifying the main message – topic sentences
>
> Students are aften required to do a large amount of reading. To save time and to select the best text(s) for your needs, it is important to identify the main message as quickly as possible.
>
> To do this:
> - look at the title.
> - quickly skim the text to find the topic sentences. They are usually the first sentence in each paragraph. They summarize what the paragraph is about.

3 Read the summaries a–d of the paragraphs in the article *The Car that Drives Itself*. Match them with topic sentences 1–4. Do not read the article.

Summaries		Topic sentences
a describing how the car works	1 ☐	A car manufacturer has designed and built a car that drives itself.
b predicting future developments	2 ☐	Despite these disadvantages, car manufacturers see driverless cars as the future.
c outlining some problems	3 ☐	However, there are still two main drawbacks.
d introducing the subject	4 ☐	The car works using two main devices.

Handwritten answers:

2
1 T   2 F   3 T   4 F   5 T   6 F

3   a 4   b 2   c 3   d 1

4
1 A   2 D   3 C   4 B

Technology Today

INNOVATIONS

THE SILENT PLANE

Annoyance from aeroplane noise could be a thing of the past as plans are announced to design a silent aircraft. The aim is to reduce the noise from a plane so that city-dwellers will no longer hear it passing overhead once it has left the airport.

This noise reduction will be achieved in three main ways. Firstly, the plane is being designed as a single, wide wing. Secondly, the engines will be placed above the wing, inside the plane, rather than under the wings and outside, and thirdly the airplane will be flown differently, for example at a reduced speed when it is near the airport.

The aircraft is just a design concept at the moment and many technological challenges will have to be met before we have silent planes overhead.

THE CAR THAT DRIVES ITSELF

A _____ It can steer itself and control its speed. This is the latest development in the long history of the automobile industry.

B _____ The first is a radar sensor in the front of the car. It scans the road in front of the car, looking for other vehicles. It then speeds the car up or slows it down according to the traffic conditions. The second device is a camera below the rear-view mirror which watches the white lines in the road. It uses these lines as a guide to steering the car.

C _____ Firstly, the system can only work on motorways, and secondly, cars still need a driver. If the driver doesn't touch the steering wheel every 10 seconds, the devices can stop working.

D _____ They are already working on new models that will be able to drive on city roads. So, perhaps one day soon, we will be able to jump into our cars and sleep or read a book as we are driven to work!

Opinions and Questions: the Readers Write!

Sir,

Is anyone else fed up with their computer? I bought one to make my life easier and it has done exactly the opposite! Everyone told me that it would be easy to set up. 'A child could do it!' they said. So, I tried and it has been a disaster. It crashes constantly and instead of saving me time, I seem to spend all my free time trying to make it work. If this is an example of modern technology, give me an old-fashioned typewriter anytime!

Yours

W.F. Campbell (Mr)

Dear Sir,

I strongly disagree with the previous correspondent about CD players being better than MP3 players. For most of us, who are busy and on-the-move, an MP3 player is ideal. It is light, portable and convenient. You can store thousands of songs on it to listen to wherever you are. What's more, most MP3 players now allow you to watch videos, look at photographs and connect to the Internet. Brilliant!

Yours faithfully,

Paula Adams

Sir,

I am writing to ask for some advice about memory sticks. I use mine to keep a copy of my data, in case something goes wrong with my computer. However, I was told that memory sticks are unreliable and are easily damaged by anything magnetic, or by going through scanners, at airports, for example. Could you please clarify for me whether this is true? I have a new job that requires me to travel regularly, and I have to take my memory stick on trips.

Yours,

A. Jefcoate

WRITING Technology – good or bad?

1 Brainstorm arguments *for* and *against* mobile phones.

Read STUDY SKILL

for	against
Can make a call at any time, anywhere.	Annoying in a public place, e.g. in a restaurant.

STUDY SKILL Organizing ideas (1)

When writing an essay where you have to give two sides of an argument:

- organize your ideas into arguments *for* and arguments *against*, and give some examples.
- write a paragraph *for*, and a paragraph *against*, giving your ideas in a logical order.
- write an introduction and a conclusion. Give your personal opinion in the conclusion.

2 Read the essay. Did you have the same ideas?

Mobile phones

A Mobile phones are now part of our everyday lives. Most people find them essential and could not manage without them. However, there are also some drawbacks to owning and using a mobile phone.

B There are three main advantages to having mobile phones. Firstly, there is the convenience of being able to make or receive a phone call at any time and in any place. Secondly, they are essential for keeping in touch with family and friends. Parents worried about their children can always ring them to check they are safe, and children can let their family know if they are going to be late home. Finally, mobile phones can save lives. For example, if there is an accident, help can be called immediately, wherever the accident takes place.

C On the other hand, there are significant problems with the use of mobile phones. In the first place, using mobile phones can cause accidents, for instance, when people are driving and using their phone at the same time. In addition, the loud use of mobile phones in public places such as restaurants and cinemas is rude and can be very irritating for other people. Lastly, there has been an increase in street crime directly related to mobile phones. People have been attacked and their phones stolen from them.

D In conclusion, I believe that, despite the disadvantages, mobile phones are essential to modern life and that the advantages of owning one are far greater than the disadvantages.

3 Consider the purpose of each paragraph. Which paragraph A, B, C, or D …?
- says why mobile phone use can be a good thing
- introduces the subject
- concludes and gives the writer's opinion
- says why mobile phone use can be a bad thing

4 **Read STUDY SKILL** Go back through the essay. Underline 12 more linking words and phrases. Write them in the table.

sequence	firstly	
contrast	in spite of	
examples	e.g.	
endings	to conclude	

STUDY SKILL Linking ideas (2)

To help the reader understand your writing and follow your ideas, link short, simple ideas. Use:
- *firstly, secondly, …*
  for more than one argument or idea
- *however* (see Study Skill p13), *on the other hand, despite …*
  for a contrast between two ideas
- *for instance, for example, …*
  for an example to illustrate an idea
- *in conclusion, to sum up, …*
  for the final comment

5 Read the essay title. Do you agree or disagree with it?
Discuss with a partner.

Access to satellite and Internet television does more harm than good.

6 Divide arguments 1–6 into those that support the essay title (*against* satellite /Internet TV), and those that disagree with it (*for* satellite/Internet TV). Add one more argument to each list.

1 People (especially children) have access to programmes with unsuitable content.
2 It gives people access to programmes around the world – the opportunity to learn about other cultures.
3 A huge choice of programmes is available – something for every interest, for example sport, music, film, documentary channels.
4 More access to TV encourages people (especially children) to watch more TV, so there is less time for hobbies or family.
5 Programmes in other languages, for example English, can support language learning.
6 The programmes available may not be culturally appropriate.

for satellite TV	against satellite TV
	The programmes available may not be culturally appropriate.

Writing a discursive essay

7 Complete the essay using the arguments from exercise 6. Link ideas with words and phrases from exercise 4. Follow the organization in the box. Write about 200 words.

Title Access to satellite and Internet television does more harm than good.

Introduction
Many people have strong feelings about the value of television, especially now that programmes are available through satellite and over the Internet. There are those who suggest that increased access to these programmes does more harm than good. However, there are those who insist that it is a good thing.

Paragraph 2   satellite and Internet TV does harm + examples

Paragraph 3   satellite and Internet TV is good + examples

Paragraph 4   conclusion and your opinion

VOCABULARY DEVELOPMENT Varying vocabulary (1)

1 Match the linking words or phrases with their synonyms.

1 ☐ finally		a	but
2 ☐ firstly		b	for instance
3 ☐ for example		c	in contrast
4 ☐ however		d	in the first place
5 ☐ in conclusion		e	lastly
6 ☐ on the other hand		f	to conclude

2 Replace the word(s) in bold in each sentence with a synonym from the box.

> drawbacks   essential   immediately   made illegal   rise

1 There are three **disadvantages** to your suggestion.
2 Smoking at work has been **outlawed** in many countries.
3 Most car owners believe their car is **necessary** for their work and leisure.
4 If there has been a car accident, you should call the police **straight away**.
5 There has been a huge **increase** in mobile phone ownership.

3 [Read STUDY SKILL] Use your dictionary to find synonyms for these words from the unit.

> ### STUDY SKILL Avoiding repetition (1)
>
> To avoid sounding repetitive in your writing, try not to use the same words too often. Where possible, use a synonym. A good dictionary will often give you a synonym within the definition of a word, or the symbol SYN next to a word with the same meaning.
>
> > ★**finally** /ˈfaɪnəli/ *adv.* **1** after a long time or delay: *It was getting dark when the plane finally took off.* [SYN] **eventually 2** used to introduce the last in a list of things: *Finally, I would like to say how much we have all enjoyed this evening.* [SYN] **lastly 3** in a definite way so that sth will not be changed: *We haven't decided finally who will get the job yet.*

> ideal   wonderful   manufacture   automobile
> accelerate   steal   rude   discover

4 Replace the words in bold in the paragraph with synonyms. Use your dictionary to help.

> Smart cards, that is, credit cards, mobile phone SIM cards, and so on, which contain a **very small** computer microprocessor, have their origins in the 1970s. A Frenchman, Roland Moreno, **manufactured** a circuit that could **store** electronic **data**. Since then, this idea has **grown** into a multi-billion-dollar **business**.

REVIEW

1 Look at the essay titles. Brainstorm and write down three arguments *for* and three arguments *against* each title.

Using computers saves a lot of time.

Cars should be banned from city centres.

Young people spend too much time playing computer games.

People have become too dependent on modern technology.

2 Write a topic sentence which states the main idea for each paragraph below.

Laptop computers

Many people now travel the world on business and they need to be able to use a computer at all times. Firstly, it is important that they can write and answer important emails when they are away from their offices. Secondly, having a laptop means that people don't waste time when they are travelling, as they can work while they are on a plane or train, for example. Lastly, a laptop can also help busy businessmen and women to relax. They can listen to music or watch their favourite movie while they are hundreds of kilometres from home!

Voice-controlled technology

Already some people have installed voice-controlled technology in their homes. They use their mobile phones to 'tell' their lights to switch on, or to 'order' their television to turn off. However, in the future more and more of us will be using this technology to control our heating, our lighting, and security in our homes. Perhaps one day we will be able to 'tell' our ovens to cook our dinners!

3 Divide the vocabulary from Unit 4 into two topics: cars and aeroplanes.

> airport   fly   motorways   plane   rear-view mirror
> steering wheel   traffic   wing

4 Add four of the words in the box to the two topics. Use your dictionary to help. Record these words in groups using a method from the Study Skill box on page 14.

> accelerator   brakes   clutch   cockpit
> emergency exit   pilot   take off   tyres

5 Conferences and visits

READING SKILLS   Purpose and audience (1) and (2)
WRITING SKILLS   Using formal expressions • Writing a formal email
VOCABULARY DEVELOPMENT   Suffixes • Prefixes

READING   A conference in Istanbul

1 Label documents a–d on page 29. Which is … ?

- an itinerary   • an informal email   • an invitation   • a programme of events

2 Work with a partner.   **Read STUDY SKILL**

1 What is the purpose of each document a–d?
2 Who is each document for?

> a passenger   a friend   a speaker at a conference

> **STUDY SKILL**   Purpose and audience (1)
>
> To understand the contents of a text better, predict what you can before you read. As well as titles, pictures, and headings think about:
> - layout, size, and style of the print.
> - purpose, for example, *to inform*, *to sell*.
> - audience (who it is written for), for example, *a student*, *an expert*.

3 Scan the documents. Answer as many questions as you can in three minutes.

The programme

Where is the conference being held?

Who is the conference for?

When does the conference start and finish?

What time does the sightseeing tour start?

What time is the *Farewell Dinner*?

The people

Who is the invitation to?

Who is the first speaker at the conference?

Who is talking about the international novel?

Who is the email to?

Who is the email from?

Dr Khuffash

What time does she leave Amman?

What time does she arrive back home in Amman?

Where does Dr Khuffash teach?

What is she looking forward to most?

4 Complete the definitions using words and phrases in bold from the documents.

1 _____ is visiting important and historic places in a city as a tourist.

2 A _____ is a meeting or talk that everyone should attend.

3 A _____ is the place where people meet for an organized event.

4 An _____ is a collection of things, for example books or paintings for people to look at.

5 A _____ _____ means someone you know, a friend.

6 _____ is saying or writing what you think is good or bad about something, for example, a book or essay.

7 To _____ _____ _____ is to wait with pleasure for something to happen.

8 The _____ of a meeting is the person in charge.

9 A _____ is someone who teaches at a university.

10 _____ is another more formal word for 'goodbye'.

NATIONAL UNIVERSITY OF TURKEY
We have pleasure in inviting *Dr Laura Khuffash* to the

3rd International Conference
for Teachers of English Language and Literature

5 October – 8 October   **Venue**: Istanbul City Hotel

Programme Day 1

9–10.30   **Plenary** Session
Chair Dr John Bryan, Head of English, University of Leeds
10.30–11.00   Coffee break and **exhibition**
11.00–13.00   Choice between:
- *English as a World Language*
Dr Laura Khuffash, Senior **Lecturer**, Birzeit University
- *English and Tourism*
Dr. Mahmoud Suhbi, Ministry of Tourism and Development, Libya
- *Novels in Translation*
Dr Meral Soyer, Lecturer, National University of Turkey
- *The International Novel*
Dr Richard Dean, Lecturer, University of West London
13.00–14.00   Lunch
14.00   Coach leaves hotel for **sightseeing** tour. Visits will include:
Hagia Sophia/Blue Mosque/Topkapi Palace
17.00   Return to hotel
20.00   Dinner

Programme Day 4

16.00   Final Plenary
Chair Dr John Bryan,
Head of English,
University of Leeds
20.00   **Farewell** Dinner

04/10/10

09.00   Check in Queen Alia International Airport, Amman

11.00   Depart flight RJ401

15.00   Arrive Ataturk International Airport, Istanbul

09/10/10

07.30   Check in Ataturk International Airport, Istanbul

10.30   Depart flight RJ402

15.40   Arrive Queen Alia International Airport, Amman

From: laura.khuffash@bz.ac.com
Date: Sat 29/9/10 07:50am
To: nancy.marshal@lon.ac.uk
Subject: Istanbul conference

Nancy,

Are you going to the conference in Istanbul next week? I'm giving a paper on the first day and chairing the plenary on the second day!! It would be great to see a **familiar face** in the audience. If not, I'll send you a copy of my paper on 'English as a World Language' and you can tell me what you think. Any **criticism** welcome! The programme looks great – we've even got some sightseeing arranged each day. I'm really **looking forward to** visiting the Blue Mosque – I've only ever seen photos of it. Don't forget to let me know if you'll be there.

Best wishes,

Laura

5 Skim extracts a–f. What type of texts are they? Label them.

- poem
- medical textbook
- history textbook
- novel
- note
- student essay

a _____

The chicken farm had been his idea, after Charles came back from the East with malaria. Work in the open air, Rivers had advised. He was paying for it now. As he left the shelter of the hedge and set off across two-acre field, a great gust of 'open air' almost lifted him off his feet.

e _____

Dysphagia This term includes both difficulty with swallowing and pain on swallowing. The former symptom is more prominent in obstruction and the latter with inflammatory lesions. The patient can sometimes point to the site of the obstruction.

b _____

Some of the features of the typical (medieval) village were inherent in the essential needs of agriculture and of social life, and may therefore appear too obvious to be worth specifying. The most obvious characteristic of the village was its topography.

c _____

A thing of beauty is a joy for ever

A thing of beauty is a joy for ever:
Its loveliness increases; it will never
Pass into nothingness: but still will keep
A bower quiet for us, and a sleep . . .

f _____

In conclusion, it is clear that the arguments in favour of reducing carbon gases through the increased use of renewable sources are stronger than those supporting the increased building of nuclear power stations.

d _____

Paul, can't come to the lecture today – not feeling well.
Can you explain to the prof. and can I look at your notes?!!

Cheers,

Tom

6 **Read STUDY SKILL** Choose a style or styles from the box to describe texts a–f in exercise 5. Underline vocabulary, phrases, and any examples of punctuation in the extracts that helped you decide.

| informal | formal | literary | academic | medical |

Extract a: a novel – literary style

STUDY SKILL Purpose and audience (2)

The choice of vocabulary, grammatical style, and punctuation of a text depends on its purpose and its expected audience.

When you are writing, think about *who* is going to read your work and *why* you are writing. Then decide what the overall style should be, for example *literary*, *academic*, *formal*, *informal*, etc.

WRITING Invitations

1 Skim emails A and B. Which is formal? Which is informal?

A

Dear Nancy,

Thanks for the invitation to your wedding. Congratulations to you both! [1]**I'd love to come.** How exciting! I've already booked flights – [2]**see attachment**.

[3]**It'd be great if you could send me the email address of the hotel you're booking me into.**

[4]**I'm really looking forward to seeing you again.**

[5]**Best wishes** (and to Mark, too!),

Laura

B

Dear Dr Bryan,

I have great pleasure in accepting your kind invitation to the 3rd International Conference for Teachers of English Language and Literature to be held in Istanbul from 5th to 8th October. Please find attached my arrival and departure details as requested.

It would be greatly appreciated if you could send me the contact details (email and telephone/fax) for the Istanbul City Hotel.

I look forward to meeting you and your colleagues in October.

Yours sincerely,

Dr Laura Khuffash

Birzeit University

2 Look at the expressions in bold in email A. Find matching expressions in email B.

I'd love to come. = I have great pleasure in accepting ...

3 Match formal phrases 1–6 with endings a–f to make full sentences. There may be more than one possible answer. **Read STUDY SKILL**

1 ☐ I am writing
2 ☐ I have pleasure
3 ☐ Please find attached
4 ☐ I look forward
5 ☐ I would like
6 ☐ Please feel free

a in attaching your programme.
b to suggest changes.
c to meeting you next month.
d your itinerary and hotel reservations.
e to welcome you to our town.
f to inform you that the conference dates have been changed.

STUDY SKILL Using formal expressions

When you write emails for academic or professional purposes, it is important to use a more formal tone. You can do this by learning fixed expressions by heart. For example:

I have great pleasure in + *-ing*
I am writing + infinitive
I would like + infinitive
Please feel free + infinitive
I look forward to + *-ing*
Please find attached/enclosed + noun

4 Work with a partner. Brainstorm things to do and see in your town.

5 An important lecturer is coming to visit to give a series of two-hour seminars at your college/university. Prepare a three-day programme to include hotel details, lectures (titles, venue, days and times), cultural and other free-time activities.

Day 1

10.00 – 12.00, 'Technology of the future'
– Lecture Theatre 2
12.30 Lunch
3.00 Visit to the National Museum

Writing a formal email

6 Write an email to your visitor (75–100 words) using some of the words and phrases in exercise 3. Include these points:

- Address your visitor.
- Tell him/her why you are writing.
- Give details of attachments (itinerary – dates and times of arrival and departure, lecture times and locations, accommodation).
- Briefly summarize the programme. Give an example of optional cultural and free-time activities. Tell the visitor that any suggestions for changes are welcome.
- Close the email appropriately.

VOCABULARY DEVELOPMENT Word-building (2)

1 Look at the words from Unit 5. Use a dictionary to identify what part of speech each word is.

> invitation   international   forget   renewable
> criticism   really   enjoy   greatly

2 Complete the table for each word with one example of each part of speech. Mark the stressed syllable. Use your dictionary to help. `Read STUDY SKILL`

verb	noun	adjective	adverb
think			
			hopefully
pain			
	pleasure		
		critical	

STUDY SKILL Suffixes

Identify the part of speech of a word (verb, noun, adjective, or adverb) to help you understand the meaning and develop your vocabulary, for example:

inform (v), *information* (n)
informal (adj), *informally* (adv)

Suffixes give you clues to the part of speech, for example:

- *-tion, -ism, -ment, -ity, -ness* are noun suffixes, for example, *invitation*
- *-al, -ful, -able* are adjective suffixes, for example, *international*
- *-ly* is an adverb suffix, for example, *formally*

3 `Read STUDY SKILL` Match meanings 1–10 with prefixes a–j. Use the example words in *italics* to help.

1 ☐ against
2 ☐ wrong; not
3 ☐ small/tiny
4 ☐ after
5 ☐ two/twice
6 ☐ under
7 ☐ across; change
8 ☐ again
9 ☐ by itself/oneself
10 ☐ many

a auto-   *autobiography*
b anti-   *antiseptic*
c bi-   *bilingual*
d micro-   *microphone*
e mis-   *misprint*
f multi-   *multimedia*
g post-   *postgraduate*
h re-   *review*
i sub-   *submarine*
j trans-   *transform*

STUDY SKILL Prefixes

Adding a prefix changes the meaning of a word. Each prefix has a different meaning and can be found as a separate entry in the dictionary. For example:

mis- means *wrong* or *not* e.g. *misunderstand*.
bi- means *two* or *twice*, e.g. *biannual* (twice a year).

(handwritten notes)
1 b   9 a
2 e   10 f
3 d
4 g
5 c
6 i
7 j
8 h

4 Complete definitions 1–10 with an example word from exercise 3.

1 To _____ is to change something completely.

2 A _____ is a piece of electrical equipment that is used for making sounds and voices louder.

3 Someone who is _____ can speak two languages equally well.

4 A liquid or cream which stops a cut becoming infected is called an _____ .

5 A type of ship which can travel underwater is a _____ .

6 To _____ your work is to look at it again to make sure you understand.

7 An _____ is the story of a person's life written by that person.

8 A _____ is someone doing further studies at a university after his or her first degree.

9 _____ is using sound, pictures, and film as well as text on a screen.

10 A _____ is a mistake in printing or typing.

REVIEW

1 Look at documents a–c and answer the questions.

1 What is each document? Label them.
2 Who do you think wrote each one?
3 Who is each one intended for?

a [   ]

Dear Dr Stone,

I am writing to apply for the William Frank Bursary in Biological Sciences at the University of West London.

I am currently in my final year of a degree in Biochemistry at Birzeit University and will graduate in July this year. Please find enclosed a reference from my tutor and a copy of my final year paper in support of my academic qualifications. ...

b [   ]

TONBRIDGE SUMMER SCHOOLS
Reference: TSS07

Temporary Social Organizer

We are looking for an energetic, friendly, and patient student who wishes to improve their English while working.

Applicants should speak Arabic fluently, and English at intermediate level or above. They should have reasonable computer skills (Word and Excel) and ...

c [   ]

TO ALL CANDIDATES:

This is a reminder that the final Chemistry examination is on Tuesday 27th May at 9a.m.

Please be at the examinations centre 15 minutes before the start of the exam. Late arrivals will not be allowed into the examination hall.

All candidates must show their university ID cards.

2 Rewrite the email to Mrs Bateman replacing the phrases in **bold** with more formal expressions.

○ ○ ○   ▭

Dear Mrs Bateman,

Thanks for your letter. **I'd really like to come** to the exhibition. **It would be great** if you could send me some information about transport between the airport and the exhibition hall. I have written a brief biography **as you asked me – see attachment**.

Really looking forward to meeting you soon.

Yours sincerely,
Frank Baker

3 Complete the paragraph with the correct form of the words in brackets. Use your dictionary to help

Dr Khuffash is ¹_____ (current) a senior ²_____ (lecture) at Birzeit University. She is an expert on the ³_____ (develop) of English as an international language. She is ⁴_____ (particular) ⁵_____ (interest) in the use of English in the fields of science and medicine. Dr Khuffash is also a noted ⁶_____ (novel) and poet.

6 Science and our world

READING SKILLS Making notes • Interpreting meaning
WRITING SKILLS Paraphrasing and summarizing • Writing a summary
VOCABULARY DEVELOPMENT Noun/Verb + preposition • Using numbers

READING Air pollution

1 What are the causes and effects of air pollution?
Discuss with a partner and make two lists.

Causes   factory emissions ...
Effects

Skim the report *Air Pollution* on page 35.
Are your ideas the same?

2 Scan the report and answer the questions.

1 What is the main cause of air pollution?
2 What are two natural sources of air pollution?
3 Which are the most polluted cities in the world?
4 Where was the first study done?
5 What health problems did the first study look at?
6 Where was the second study done?
7 What health problem did the second study look at?

3 Scan the report again. What do the numbers in the box refer to?

| 20 | three times | two | 25,000 | 250 | second | 2.5 |

4 Read the notes and compare them to the highlighted and
underlined sections in paragraph 1 of the report. **Read STUDY SKILL**

Air pollution – major problem
Man-made causes   **Natural causes**
- vehicles – major cause   • volcanoes
- power stations   • forest fires
- factories
- mining/building
- burning – fossil fuels/wood
∴ more cars = more pollution in major cities

5 Make notes from the underlined information in paragraph 2.

6 Read paragraph 3 carefully and highlight the key information.

7 Write about paragraph 3 from the prompts in the box.

| Where ...? | What ... studied? | Who ...? |
| How many ...? | Where ... live? | What results ...? |

STUDY SKILL Making notes

Take time to make good notes. They will help you to
organize, record, and remember important information
you have read. Use your notes to prepare for essay
writing, for doing revision, and for sitting exams.

To find and mark relevant information:
- ask yourself what information you need.
- read and underline/highlight relevant information in
  the text (use different colours to represent different
  types of information, for example, blue for *man-
  made causes*, yellow for *natural causes*).
- rewrite the information as notes.

To organize your notes:
- use bullet points, headings, and numbering.

To be concise:
- don't write full sentences. Leave out words that are
  not central to understanding/meaning:
  articles (*a, an, the*)   the verb *'to be'*
  prepositions (*in, at, on*)   auxiliary verbs (*has* sent)
- Use some simple abbreviations and symbols:
  e.g. (*for example*)   ∴ (*therefore*)
  ∵ (*because*)   = (*equals/means*)
  → (*leads to*)

Air pollution

Air pollution is a major problem all over the world today. Probably the single biggest contributor to the problem is the motor vehicle. However, there are many other man-made sources, such as industrial factories, power stations, mining, building, and the burning of fossil fuels and wood in homes around the world. There are natural sources of air pollution too; volcanoes and forest fires produce a lot of pollutants. However, it is the increasing number and use of motor vehicles that is doing the most damage, and logically, where there are more cars, there is more pollution, that is, in the major cities of the world. Some of the most polluted cities include Beijing, Mexico City, Athens, Moscow, and Mumbai.

Health problem

This problem of increased pollution in the major cities of the world has led to an increase in the number of studies done to look at the effects on our health. The results so far are not very reassuring. In fact, air pollution may be a much greater danger to our health than scientists believed before. A 20-year study of residents of a Cairo suburb shows that the tiny particles in polluted air could lead to three times as many long-term health problems as was previously thought. A connection between the number of particles in the air and health is suggested by Dr Razia of Cairo University. He and his colleagues collected data on 25,000 residents of Cairo over two decades. They found that as the number of tiny particles, those less than 2.5 microns in diameter, increased, so did the risk of dying from health problems such as heart attacks and lung cancer.

Traffic and asthma

Other studies show a similar link between traffic pollution and ill health. A second group of researchers in Ottawa, Canada, reported that children living near busy roads were more likely to develop asthma. They studied the health of 250 children in different Canadian cities. The results suggest a strong connection between how close a child lives to traffic and the possibility of that child developing asthma and other similar diseases.

It is clear from these studies and others that the time has come to start reducing the levels of air pollution in our cities for the sake of our children and future generations.

---

8 **Read STUDY SKILL** Read the report again. Are the statements expressed as fact (**F**) or speculation (**S**) in the text?

1 Growing car use is causing the most damage. **F**
2 More pollution in big cities has resulted in more studies being done.
3 Polluted air is more dangerous than people thought.
4 Small particles in dirty air cause three times as many health problems.
5 The results of the Canadian studies prove there is a link between a child living close to traffic and getting asthma.
6 All these studies show that it is important to reduce air pollution for the next generation.

STUDY SKILL Interpreting meaning

Most academic and scientific articles express facts (what happened), and speculate (guess). It is important to be able to distinguish uncertainty and speculation from fact.

Uncertainty and speculation can be expressed using:

- *may, could, might* before the main verb, e.g.
  *Air pollution **may be** a much greater danger to our health …*
  *Polluted air **could** lead to three times as many … problems.*
- verbs such as *believe, claim, think, hope, seem*, e.g.
  *Dr Razia … **believes** there is a connection between the number of particles in the air and health.*
- words and phrases, e.g.
  possibly, probably, it is possible

1 Read the report *School dinner scandal*. Underline the main information.

Report

School dinner scandal

The results of a study into what 10,000 primary school children, that is, children aged five to eleven, ate in a day shocked the researchers. They believe it shows that children's diets are getting worse and that this might cause health problems in the future. It shows that 49 per cent of the children had eaten chips, which had been cooked in oil. Less than half had eaten a vegetable or a piece of fruit in the last 24 hours and, most shockingly, only one in ten children had eaten fish.

As Dr G. Bennett, the author of the study, concluded (2006, p191), 'Poor eating habits in early childhood can lead to health problems in later life. It is therefore essential to ensure that children eat properly.'

2 Read the summary. Match the highlighted words and phrases with words and phrases in the report.

Research = a study

Summary

Research into 10,000 primary pupils' daily diet revealed that just under half had eaten chips, fewer than 50% had had either vegetables or fruit, and only 10% of the children had eaten fish.

3 Read the article *Scientists on the decline* on page 37. Highlight or underline the main information.

4 Make notes from the information you have highlighted or underlined. Organize them logically, and be concise.

Number science students ↓ about 5% a year.

Scientists on the decline

As science becomes increasingly important in our daily lives, so the shortage of scientists gets greater. The number of students going to university to study pure and applied sciences is decreasing by about five per cent each year. This, in turn, leads to a drop in the number of people able to be science teachers in schools. This shortage of science teachers, unsurprisingly, leads to fewer school children studying science, and even fewer going on to university. Prominent scientists believe that one of the reasons is that science is undervalued in society; people do not discuss the latest scientific breakthrough in the same way they would discuss the latest bestseller. It could also be because scientists starting their professional lives are often poorly paid. However, some scientists think that the reason is a distrust of scientists because of the claims for 'breakthroughs' and 'cures' for diseases which do not actually happen. Whatever the reason, young people must be encouraged to study science. The world needs scientists.

5 **Read STUDY SKILL** Write sentences in your own words using your notes. Do not look back at the text *Scientists on the decline*.

There is an annual fall of around five per cent in the number of people studying science in higher education.

STUDY SKILL Paraphrasing and summarizing

You often need to use other sources, for example other people's work, in your own essays and reports.

This can be done by:
- paraphrasing information, that is, rewriting information in your own words. Use synonyms wherever possible (see Study Skill p26).
- summarizing the information, that is, linking the main points in your own words.

NOTE   You may quote directly from the piece of work, but it is essential to give the source of the quote and its author, e.g.

… Dr G. Bennett, the author of the study, concluded (2006, p191) 'Poor eating habits in early childhood can lead to health problems in later life.'

The use of other people's work 'word for word' without saying you have done so (plagiarizing) is strictly not allowed.

Writing a summary

6 Use your sentences in exercise 5 to write a paragraph (50–75 words) summarizing the text.

VOCABULARY DEVELOPMENT

Words that go together

1 **Read STUDY SKILL** Scan the texts in the unit to find the prepositions that go with the nouns.

1 a source _of_

2 the problem _____

3 an increase _____

4 a connection _____

5 a link _____

6 a level _____

7 a shortage _____

8 a distrust _____

> **STUDY SKILL** Noun/Verb + preposition
>
> To use a word correctly, it is necessary to know the words which are associated with it, e.g.
>
> noun + preposition   a connection *between*
> verb + preposition   to die *from*
>
> When you look up a new word in the dictionary, remember to note the preposition(s) that go with it. The example sentences will help you choose the correct preposition.

2 Complete the sentences with the correct preposition. Scan the texts or use a dictionary to help.

1 Increased pollution may lead _____ more illness.

2 Forest fires can contribute _____ an increase in air pollution.

3 Some cyclists wear face masks to protect themselves _____ pollution.

4 The number of maths students has decreased _____ six per cent.

5 Scientists are looking _____ ways to encourage more people to study science.

Using numbers

3 The numbers in the box are taken from the texts in the unit. Can you remember what they represent?

25,000	2.5	49%	one in ten

4 **Read STUDY SKILL** Match numbers 1–10 to facts a–j. Compare your answers with a partner.

1 ☐ The average temperature of a human is …

2 ☐ The coldest recorded temperature on Earth is …

3 ☐ The population of China is …

4 ☐ The height of Mount Everest in metres is …

5 ☐ The amount of the Earth that is covered by sea is …

6 ☐ The average number of hairs on a person's head is …

7 ☐ The value of the mathematical symbol pi (π) is …

8 ☐ The approximate distance to the moon is …

9 ☐ The number of Arabic speakers in the world is …

10 ☐ The number of bytes in a gigabyte is …

a 8,850 metres

b 37°C

c 110,000

d 382,500 km

e 1,306,313,812

f 1 billion

g 3.14159265

h 70%

i -89.4°C

j 174,950,000

> **STUDY SKILL** Using numbers
>
> Numbers are frequently used in academic and professional writing and speaking.
>
> **Cardinal numbers**, e.g. 22, 407, 2,056, 1,345,644
> Use a comma to separate millions and thousands.
>
> | Five billion/million/ thousand/hundred | five million (not millions) |
> |---|---|
> | 407 | four hundred and seven. |
> | 3,476 | three thousand, four hundred and seventy-six |
>
> **Ordinal numbers**
> first/1st   second/2nd   third/3rd, etc.
>
> **Ratios, decimals, percentages, and temperatures**
>
> | 1:5 | a ratio of one to five |
> |---|---|
> | 62%. | sixty-two per cent (not per cents) |
> | 0.7 | nought /nɔːt/ point seven |
> | ¼ ⅓ ½ ¾ | a quarter, a third, a half, three quarters |
> | 6.05 | six point oh five |
> | −5°C | five degrees (Celsius/centigrade) below zero minus five degrees (Celsius/centigrade) |

REVIEW

1 Read the three texts. Highlight facts in blue and speculation in pink.

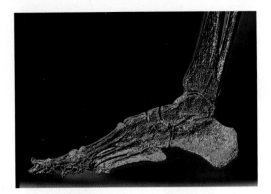

Old shoes

Scientists believe the first shoes were worn about 30,000 years ago. When shoes are worn, the toe bones get weaker. There is evidence that humans 30,000 years ago had toes which were weaker than those of their ancestors. This, the scientists claim, is because they started wearing shoes.

Bright veggies

Brightly-coloured fruit and vegetables, like carrots and oranges, could protect against diseases such as arthritis. These vegetables and fruit contain vitamin C and other elements which work against the disease. So, if you enjoy eating lots of oranges, you could also be helping your body to fight disease.

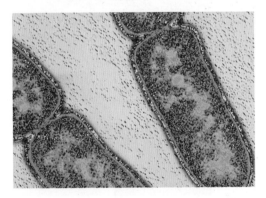

The ancient origins of tuberculosis

Scientists used to believe tuberculosis (TB) was just tens of thousands of years old, but studies of ancient skeletons suggest the disease existed in East Africa three million years ago. Scientists hope to use this new information in their fight against TB, as this disease kills three million people a year.

2 Use a dictionary to find prepositions that go with the verbs and nouns.

verbs		nouns	
apply	___	reason	___
concentrate	___	demand	___
consist	___	cause	___
depend	___	solution	___
search	___	rise	___
suffer	___	reaction	___

3 Correct the mistakes in the sentences.
1 Today is his forty birthday.
2 More than 6 millions people watched the final.
3 There was an increase of five point two nought six.
4 They received a pay rise of four per cents.
5 Today's temperature is 7 degrees under zero.

7 People: past and present

READING SKILLS Using original sources
RESEARCH Using the Internet • Developing a search plan
WRITING SKILLS Adding extra information • Organizing ideas (2) • Writing from research

READING Three famous writers

1 Think of two books you have read recently. Who wrote them? What were they about? Why did you read them? Discuss with a partner.

2 Look quickly at extracts a–g on page 41. Which ones are about … ?

☐☐ William Shakespeare   ☐☐ Agatha Christie   ☐☐☐ Ahmed Shawqi

3 Scan the extracts and complete the notes in the chart. **Read STUDY SKILL**

STUDY SKILL Using original sources

Decide what information you need from a source. Scan the text to find the relevant part.

Original sources often have difficult language and unknown vocabulary, so don't worry about not understanding *everything*. You can:

- guess the meaning of unknown words from context (See Study Skill p17).
- use a dictionary.
- try a different source.

	Shakespeare	Agatha Christie	Ahmed Shawqi
country			
born			
early life and family			
profession			
famous for			
death			

4 Match the dictionary definitions with the words in bold from the texts.

1 A _____ is someone who writes poetry.

2 If a subject is _____-_____ , there is very little written information about it.

3 A _____ is a book that is bought by a very large number of people.

4 If you have a book _____ , you have it prepared and printed for sale.

5 A _____ is a play that has a sad ending.

6 An _____ is someone who writes books.

7 A _____ is someone who writes plays.

8 A _____ is a play or film that makes you laugh.

William Shakespeare

Agatha Christie

Ahmed Shawqi

a William Shakespeare (1564–1616), English **playwright** and poet, recognized in much of the world as the greatest of all dramatists ... For someone who lived almost 400 years ago, a surprising amount is known about Shakespeare's life. Indeed we know more about his life than about almost any other writer of his age ...

Shakespeare wrote nearly all of his plays from 1590 to 1611. The great **tragedies** – including Hamlet, Othello, King Lear, and Macbeth – were written during the first decade of the 1600s. Shakespeare died on April 23, 1616.

b Ahmad Shawqi was born in Cairo in 1868 to a middle class family which was related to the royal family. He was raised by his grandmother ...

c Agatha Christie (1890–1976), British **author** of mystery novels and short stories, is especially famous as the creator of Hercule Poirot, the Belgian detective, and Miss Jane Marple.

Agatha Christie was born in Torquay, in the county of Devon. Her father died when she was a child. Christie was educated at home, where her mother encouraged her to write from a very early age. At sixteen she was sent to school in Paris where she studied singing and piano.

In 56 years Christie wrote 66 detective novels, among the best of which are The Murder of Roger Acroyd, Murder On The Orient Express (1934), Death On The Nile (1937) ...

In 1967 Christie became president of the British Detection Club, and in 1971 she was made a Dame of the British Empire. Christie died on January 12, 1976. With over one hundred novels and 103 translations into foreign languages, Christie was by the time of her death the best-selling English novelist of all time.

d Ahmed Shawqi (1868–1932) (Arabic: ____ ____); Egyptian **poet** and dramatist ... Shawqi produced distinctive poetry that is widely considered to be the most prominent of the 20th century Arabic literary movement.

... his family was well-connected with the court of the Khedive of Egypt. He attended law school, obtaining a degree in translation. Shawqi was then offered a job in the court of the Khedive Abbas II, which he immediately accepted. After a year working in the court of the Khedive, Shawqi was sent to continue his studies in Law at the Universities of Montpellier and Paris for three years.

Plays
Shawqi was the first in Arabic literature to write poetic plays. He wrote five tragedies ... and two **comedies**.

Poetry
Ash-Shawqiyyat, his selected works, in four volumes, includes Nahj al-Burda, a tribute to the prophet Muhammed.

e Ahmed Shawqi is known as 'the poet of Arabism and Islam'.

His collection of poetry, Al Shawkiyat, **published** initially in 1890, remains a classic of Islamic literature.

His family's connection to Khedive's palace led him to spend his early life in luxurious conditions. After completing his education in law in Paris in 1893 and spending an additional six months in France, he returned to Egypt. Celebrating the publishing of the second edition of Al Shawkiyat, in April 1927, Shawki was named Poet Laureate of Egypt.

f Shakespeare's reputation as dramatist, poet, and actor is unique ... Sadly his life-story remains **ill-documented**. We do know that Shakespeare was born in Stratford-upon-Avon in Warwickshire, England, and that he was probably educated in the town's free grammar school. Then in 1582 he married Anne Hathaway.

The first collected edition of Shakespeare's works was published after his death in 1623 and is known as the First Folio. The plays fall into the categories of history, tragedy, comedy, and tragicomedy.

g Agatha Christie (1890–1976), English novelist, who was a prolific writer of mystery stories. She was born in Torquay. The Mysterious Affair at Styles (1920) began her career. Hercule Poirot is the hero of many of her works, including the classic **bestseller** The Murder of Roger Ackroyd (1926).

In 1930, while travelling in the Middle East, Christie met the noted English archaeologist Sir Max Mallowan. They were married that year, and from that time on Christie accompanied her husband on annual trips to Iraq and Syria.

In 1971 she was made a Dame Commander of the Order of the British Empire.

RESEARCH Information on the Net

1 Read the two extracts about Shakespeare. What do you :

`Read STUDY SKILL`

> **1** For someone who lived almost 400 years ago, a surprising amou~~n~~... ~~a~~bout Shakespeare's life. Indeed we know more about his life than about almost any other w~~riter of the time~~.
>
> **2** Sadly, his life-story remains ill-documented.

STUDY SKILL Using the Internet

The Internet is a huge resource, so get to know different types of sites for finding information.

- **Search engines**: www.google.com, www.yahoo.com to find a fact, such as *the boiling point of mercury*.

  Some sites, www.uk.ask.com, for example, are designed so that you type in a question, such as *What is the boiling point of mercury?*

- **Online encyclopaedias**: www.wikipedia.org, www.britannica.com for more complete factual information, such as *the lifecycle of a mosquito*.

- **Subject directories**: www.bubl.ac.uk, www.rdn.ac.uk for specialist online and written resources linked to a specific subject (economics, history, etc.) such as *World History 500–1799 + country*.

Remember that information from websites is not always reliable, so check information on two or more sites.

---

2 `Read STUDY SKILL` Look at the three questions. Use a search engine to find the answers.

1 What is Chopin famous for?
   (Search: **Chopin**)

2 When did Jane Austen write *Persuasion*?
   (Search first: **Jane Austen**, search second: *Persuasion*)

3 What is Angola's main export?
   (Search phrase: **Angola's main export**)

STUDY SKILL Developing a search plan

To make an Internet search more efficient and reliable, develop a search plan.

Ask yourself questions:
- What is the general search topic?
- What information do I need to find out?
- What keywords and phrases will help me?

List the keywords and phrases in order of importance.

---

3 What type of Internet site would answers questions 1–6? Identify and underline the keywords, and then look up the information. Compare answers from at least two different sites. Is the information the same?

1 What is the average summer temperature in Amman?
2 How far is the Sun from the Earth?
3 When was the English author Charles Dickens born?
4 What percentage of the human body is water?
5 What is the average rainfall in the Amazon in May and December?
6 What are the main stages of the life cycle of a butterfly?

4 Read the notes about the two famous people. Three facts about each person are incorrect. Can you guess which ones?

5 Use the Internet to find and correct the mistakes. Underline key words or phrases to search for.

Marie Curie – born in France – 1867.
- the first woman to win two Nobel Prizes.
- famous for discovery, with husband Pierre, of radium – couple got the Nobel Prize for Peace in 1903.
- after husband's death continued working – 1921, won the Nobel Prize for Chemistry.

Zinédine Zidane – born – 1975 – Paris, France.
- one of the best footballers of all time – played for France many times.
- scored two goals in 1998 World Cup Final v. Argentina (France won 3–0), and one goal in 2006 World Cup Final.
- retired from professional football after the 2006 World Cup.

WRITING Biographies

1 Read the biography of Roger Federer. Answer the questions.

1 When and where was he born?
2 When did he win his first 'Grand Slam' title?
3 Which three competitions did he win in 2004?
4 Who has also won five Wimbledon finals in a row?
5 What is the name of Federer's special project?

Roger Federer is probably the best and most famous tennis player in the world today. He was born in Basle, in Switzerland in 1981. His parents, [1] _____ , encouraged him to start playing tennis when he was eight years old. He won his first Wimbledon title, the Wimbledon Junior, at the age of sixteen. Over the next few years he played all over the world, including in Australia, [2] _____ .

However, it was in the year 2003 that he really began to show just how good he was. He started the year by winning two tournaments in a row, in Dubai and Marseilles. He also won his first Grand Slam title at the Wimbledon Championships. In 2004 he won three out of four Grand Slam titles, in the Australian Open, Wimbledon, and the US Open. In 2007 he equalled Björn Borg's record of winning Wimbledon five times in a row. Federer went on to win the title for a sixth time in 2009. When he is not playing tennis, Federer is busy with his special project, the Roger Federer Foundation,
[3] _____ . He is also a Goodwill Ambassador to Unicef, which also helps poor children around the world.

2 Here is some extra information about the tennis player. Write it in the correct place in the text. **Read STUDY SKILL**

- where he represented Switzerland in the 2000 Olympics Games
- which helps disadvantaged children
- who met when Roger's father was in South Africa on business

STUDY SKILL Adding extra information

One way of adding extra information is to use a non-defining relative clause.
- *Roger Federer is a very famous tennis player. He was born in Basle.*
- *Roger Federer, **who was born in Basle**, is a very famous tennis player.*
- *Roger Federer, **who is a very famous tennis player**, was born in Basle.*

Use commas and relative pronouns *who* (for people), *which* (for things and animals), and *where* (for places, but omit 'there').
Basle is a city in Switzerland. Roger Federer was born there.
*Basle, **where Roger Federer was born**, is a city in Switzerland.*

3 Join the two sentences using a relative clause with *who*, *which*, or *where*.

1 Arthur Conan Doyle was a Scottish doctor. He wrote the Sherlock Holmes stories.

_____

2 The film *Amadeus* is about the life of Mozart. It won eight Oscars.

_____

3 Stratford-upon-Avon is a beautiful little town. Shakespeare was born there.

_____

4 ▐ **Read STUDY SKILL** ▐ Put the biographical information about Nelson Mandela into chronological order.

> **STUDY SKILL** Organizing ideas (2)
>
> Always consider carefully the most appropriate way to organize the information in your writing.
>
> When writing a biography, for example, it is usual to follow a chronological order, that is, time order.

Nelson Mandela – most famous politician in the world

- actively involved in the African National Congress and the fight against apartheid – the separation of black and white people
- became first democratically elected president of South Africa in 1994
- Mandela – born in South Africa in 1918 – became the most famous statesman in the world
- retired from politics in 2004, moved back to Qunu – he was born there
- was released from prison after 27 years in 1990, won the Nobel Peace Prize – shared with President de Klerk

5 Use the information from exercise 4 to write a short biography of Mandela (approximately 100 words). Use relative pronouns.

Writing from research

6 Write a biography of a famous person from your academic field or from your country (150 words). Research five central facts: birth, early life, career, what he/she is most famous for, what he/she is doing today, and add extra information.

REVIEW Organizing vocabulary (2)

1 Use words and phrases from the website extracts on page 41 to complete the sentences.

1 The life of the philosopher Socrates is _____ , so there are very few facts about him.

2 Molière is a famous French _____ . One of his most famous plays is *The Miser*.

3 *Hamlet* is an example of a _____ . It has an unhappy ending.

4 This book is _____ by Oxford University Press.

5 Vikram Seth is a famous Indian _____ . He has written many books.

6 Airport bookshops often only sell _____ , the most popular and widely-read books.

7 John Keats is a famous British _____ . His most famous poem is *To Autumn*.

8 I prefer to see _____ at the theatre because they make me laugh.

2 Copy the diagram *The Arts*. Write the topic vocabulary in the box under the correct heading in your diagram. **Read STUDY SKILL**

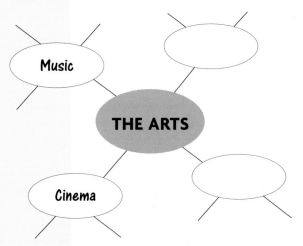

> ## STUDY SKILL Topic vocabulary
>
> Keep a vocabulary notebook or computer file and give each page a topic title, e.g. the arts, technology, etc.
>
> Record all new words of the same topic together on one page.

a composer	a conductor	a director	a landscape	a movie
a novel	a portrait	a role	a sculpture	a short story
a songwriter	a star	an abstract	an actor	an art gallery
an author	jazz	opera	poetry	prose

3 Complete sentences 1–8 with the verbs in the box.

composed	conducted	designed	directed
painted	played	starred	wrote

1 Lord Norman Foster _____ the Millau Viaduct, the highest bridge in the world.

2 Charles Dickens _____ many novels.

3 Alfred Hitchcock _____ thrillers.

4 Verdi _____ many famous operas.

5 Harrison Ford _____ in adventure films.

6 Van Gogh _____ *The Sunflowers* and many other famous pictures.

7 Scott Joplin _____ the piano.

8 Sir Georg Solti _____ the London Philharmonic Orchestra.

4 What are the comments about? Use the vocabulary in exercise 2.

1 It's about ten metres tall, made of a black metal, and stands in City Square.

2 It's just lots of circles of different colours. A child could have done it.

3 The lead actor was great and the special effects were brilliant.

4 I couldn't stop until the last page. It was so exciting.

5 It was all in Italian, so I didn't understand the words, but the music was beautiful.

8 The world of IT

READING Computers

1 Discuss with a partner how often you use a computer to:

- download music/games/films
- send an email
- write an essay
- do research
- shop on line

2 Read the description of a computer. Label the diagrams using the words in the box.

CPU	CD/DVD burner	USB port
VDU (monitor)	mouse	keyboard	scanner
printer	webcam	memory stick	speakers

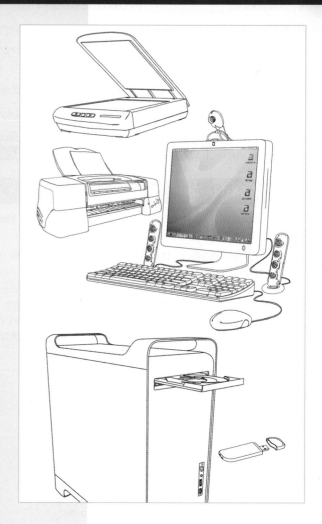

A computer is made up of several main parts. Obviously, the most important is the CPU, or central processing unit. This is the part that houses the computer memory and processing chips, in other words, the computer's brain. Most CPUs now have a CD and/or DVD burner, that is, a device for recording onto a CD or DVD, already built into the unit. They also have USB ports, that is to say, sockets where you plug in other devices, e.g. your scanner or memory stick. Most CPUs have software, i.e. computer programs, already loaded when you buy the computer, but many people like to add other programs to personalize their computer. Other necessary parts of any computer system are the monitor or screen, the mouse, and the keyboard.

3 [Read STUDY SKILL] Underline seven ways of rephrasing, explaining, and giving examples in the description in exercise 2.

STUDY SKILL Rephrasing and explaining

In technological or scientific texts, some words are often rephrased or explained:

... a CD burner,	**that is,** **i.e.**	*a device for recording onto CD.*
... hardware,	**in other words,** **or**	*the machinery of a computer.*

Sometimes an example is given instead. Look out for:

... software	**e.g.** **for example** **for instance**	*anti-virus programs, ...*

Computers under attack

Every time you turn on your computer and connect to the Internet, there is a possibility of attack! It could come via an email from a friend, a software program or music you download, or even from a CD-ROM you are using.

The most common source of danger is a 'virus', that is, a program that hides itself in documents or software, and then attacks your computer. Sometimes, **these** are not too serious. They can even be funny, but sometimes they are so serious that they crash the computer, in other words, they stop the computer working. Consequently, some companies and even government departments have had to close while **they** try to find and destroy a virus. **This** can cost millions of dollars. 5

One type of virus, known as a 'Trojan Horse', is designed to get your credit card details or bank passwords. Once **it** has this information, **it** is sent to organizations that steal your money from your bank or use your credit card to buy things. 10

Another danger is 'spyware'. Like the Trojan Horse, it hides inside your computer so that you don't know **it** is there. It might not do any damage, but it collects information about you, for example, what you buy online or what music you download. It then sends this to commercial companies.

A more common, but less dangerous, problem is 'spam', or unwanted advertising. When **it** first appeared, nobody worried about it, but now it is out of control: more than 50% of all email messages in the world are junk mail, or spam. Unfortunately, some people are now using spam to trick people and to get money from them. **This** is called 'phishing'. The simplest phishing trick is to send an email promising that you will get rich. However, to get this money, you must first send your bank details. Of course, they take the money from your bank and you certainly don't get rich! 15

20

Therefore, next time you're online, make sure your anti-virus program is up-to-date and never give anyone your bank details!

---

4 Read the article *Computers under attack*. Match terms 1–5 with definitions a–e.

1 ☐ phishing
2 ☐ spam
3 ☐ spyware
4 ☐ Trojan horse
5 ☐ virus

a a hidden program that can destroy data
b a program that can be designed to steal personal information from your computer
c advertising emails
d a program that steals money by tricking people into giving away personal information
e a program that is hidden and can be used to get information about users' online buying habits

5 What do the pronouns refer to? Look back at the article. Complete the table. **Read STUDY SKILL**

pronoun		refers to
it	(line 1)	possibility of an attack
these	(line 5)	
they	(line 8)	
This	(line 8)	
it	(line 10)	
it	(line 10)	
it	(line 13)	
it	(line 15)	
This	(line 18)	

STUDY SKILL Avoiding repetition (2)

Pronouns are used instead of repeating the same words. Understanding what pronouns refer to helps you understand a text.

- *it* replaces a singular noun or noun phrase, e.g.
  I bought a new computer. ~~The new computer~~ **It** was expensive.
- *they* replaces a plural noun or noun phrase, e.g.
  I bought some new computer games. ~~The new computer games~~ **They** are great fun.
- *this* summarizes previous information and adds new information, e.g.
  You should install an anti-virus program. ~~Installing an antivirus program~~ **This** will protect your computer.

Using pronouns also makes a text more cohesive, or connected.

WRITING IT – benefits and drawbacks

1 Read the paragraph *The benefits of wireless technology* slowly and carefully. Use the information to complete the notes.

The benefits of wireless technology

A breakthrough in computer design could lead to computer technology being available in the poorest parts of the world. An IT company has developed a laptop computer that will only cost $100. It has all the functions of an ordinary computer including WiFi and 1GB of storage. Since the price will be low, the designers hope that the laptop will be available to children in poorer parts of the world. The computer is powered by turning a handle and, as a result, it does not need an electricity supply or batteries. This should make it even more attractive to schools in the developing world.

> Wind-up _____
>
> IT company → _____ $100
>
> Low price ∴ good for children in _____ countries
>
> All functions e.g. WiFi / 1GB storage
>
> Powered _____ ∴ no electricity _____ required

2 Write simple sentences using the completed notes from exercise 1. Do not look back at the paragraph.

An IT company has produced a laptop for just $100.

3 [Read STUDY SKILL] Link the sentences using the words and phrases in brackets.

1 Many people do not back up their computer files.
They lose a lot of data.   (so)
2 Many users don't empty their mailboxes.
They may have problems downloading their mail.   (As a result)
3 There is a serious threat from viruses.
Many people install an anti-virus program.   (because)
4 Many employees do not know how to use basic programs effectively.
Many companies offer IT training.   (Consequently)
5 People use copies of programs.
Manufacturers put in secret codes to detect copies.   (since)

4 Link your sentences from exercise 2 using words and phrases from the Study Skill box.

Writing from notes

5 [Read STUDY SKILL] Use the notes to write a paragraph about computer crime.

The number of computers and computer networks has grown enormously over the past few years. Consequently, ...

> ### Computer Crime
>
> 1 Number computer networks ↑ ∴ opportunity for crime ↑
>
> 2 Number people buying online ↑ = ↑ criminals steal (e.g credit cards)
>
> 3 IT experts make networks secure ∴ criminal gangs hire own experts
>
> 4 ∴ need ↑ online security + better systems to protect users

STUDY SKILL Linking ideas (3)

To connect ideas that show the cause and result, use linking words and phrases.

- For **cause**, use *because, as, since*:
  *People in some parts of the world cannot afford computers **since/as/because** they are too expensive.*
- For **result**, use *as a result, consequently, therefore, so*:
  *He didn't have an antivirus program, and **as a result**, a virus attacked his computer.*
  *Computer scientists have tried hard to stop spam. **Consequently**, the senders of spam have become more sophisticated.*
  *TV in the UK will be digital in 2012. **Therefore**, everyone will have to buy a digital receiver.*
  *Batteries are too expensive, **so** the computer is powered by solar energy.*

STUDY SKILL
Coherent writing

To write up your notes in a natural and coherent style:
- make good notes (see Study Skill p34)
- write simple sentences, and join them using linking words and phrases (see Study Skill pp13, 24, and 48)
- use synonyms and pronouns to avoid repetition (see Study Skill pp26 and 47)

VOCABULARY DEVELOPMENT *e.g.,* etc.

1 **Read STUDY SKILL** Match abbreviations 1–8 with their meanings a–h. Check your answers in a dictionary.

1	☐ e.g.	a	and more of the same
2	☐ c. or ca.	b	for example
3	☐ cf.	c	page or pages
4	☐ i.e.	d	make a note/remember
5	☐ ibid.	e	that is
6	☐ N.B.	f	about/approximately
7	☐ p. or pp.	g	compare this with …
8	☐ etc.	h	a reference to a source (book or website) referred to previously

STUDY SKILL Abbreviations (1)

There are many common abbreviations that are used in academic and technical texts. Understanding their meaning will help you to understand the text itself better.

e.g.
c. or ca.
cf. i.e.
ibid N.B.
p. or pp.
etc.

2 Complete the sentences using abbreviations from exercise 1.

1 People now listen to music in a wide variety of ways, such as on a personal stereo, iPod, podcasts, _____ .

2 The world population today is _____ six billion people.

3 There are several other problems involved in computer programming (see _____ 173).

4 There are several career options for graduates in biochemistry, _____ working in the pharmaceutical industry.

5 _____ The library closes at 23.00.

3 Use a dictionary or the Internet to find out what the computer abbreviations stand for. Write how to say each abbreviation. **Read STUDY SKILL**

STUDY SKILL Abbreviations (2)

Some abbreviations are said as individual letters, e.g. BBC.

Some are acronyms, that is, said as words, e.g. OPEC /ˈəʊpek/.

Check in your dictionary how to say the abbreviations.

1	CPU	central processing unit	/siːpiːˈjuː/
2	CD	_____	_____
3	CD-ROM	_____	_____
4	RAM	_____	_____
5	WiFi	_____	_____
6	GB	_____	_____
7	www	_____	_____
8	R/W	_____	_____
9	USB	_____	_____
10	user ID	_____	_____
11	IP	_____	_____
12	VDU	_____	_____

4 Which abbreviations in exercises 1 and 3 are acronyms?

RESEARCH Crediting sources

1 **Read STUDY SKILL** Look carefully at the book references. Are the statements true (**T**) or false (**F**)?

> Curnick, L. (2005). <u>Biology Made Easy.</u> Crawford Press.
> Marsden, P. (2004). *Life in Rural Egypt.* Axminster University Press.

1 There is a comma after the author's family name.
2 The author's first name is written in full.
3 There is a full stop after the author's initial.
4 The year of publication is in brackets.
5 There is a comma after the year of publication.
6 The title of the book can be underlined or written in italics.
7 There is a full stop after the title of the book.
8 There is a comma at the end of the reference.

STUDY SKILL Acknowledgements

Writing an essay often involves using information taken from other sources, e.g. books or websites. It is important to acknowledge these sources in a bibliography at the end of your essay.

Styles vary in different departments. Check your department's style and use the same.

For books:

- list the sources by author's surname in alphabetical order.
- give the author's name, the title, the publisher, the year of publication.
- use the same order and punctuation for each reference.

For websites:

- give the author's name if known.
- give the title of an article in inverted commas and underline or italicize the source of the work.
- give the full address.
- give the date you accessed the web page in brackets.

2 Write out the references as entries in a bibliography.

The Greatest Inventions of All Time	John Reading	Axminster Uni. Press	2001
I is for Information	Helen Campbell	Uni. of Ashford Press	2005
A History of the Periodic Table	Fern Daniell	Crawford Press	2004
A Student's Guide to Study Skills	Christine Dix	Edinburgh Book Press	2001
What is Information Technology?	Simon Naylor	Rogers and Sons	2005

3 Look carefully at the website acknowledgement. Notice the style.

> "Avicenna" <u>Wikipedia, The Free Encyclopedia</u> http://en.wikipedia.org/wiki/Ibn_Sina (15 June 2006)

Find and correct one style mistake in each of the web references 1–3.

> **1**
> "History Trail: Archaeology" BBC
> http://www.bbc.co.uk/history/lj/archaeologylj/preview/shtml (1 May 2006)

> **2**
> "Periodic Table" <u>Webelements</u>
> <u>http://www.webelements.com/</u> (6 November 2006)

> **3**
> "United Arab Emirates" <u>WorldAtlas.com</u> http://worldatlas.com/webimage/countries/asia/ae.htm 22 October 2006

REVIEW

1 Read the three paragraphs. Draw arrows from the pronouns in bold to the noun or noun phrase they refer to.

Ⓐ Digital television UK

Although the UK government only plans to have switched completely to digital television by 2012, **it** recommends that people switch to **it** now, if they can. The best way to get digital TV is to buy a stand-alone receiver. **This** connects to most modern televisions via an aerial on the roof.

Ⓑ Laser dentistry

Very few people enjoy going to the dentist. However, the latest laser drills are extremely accurate. **They** are also nearly painless. Dentists find **them** very easy and efficient to use, and **they** say that patients are much more relaxed during treatment.

Ⓒ The Death of Guide Books

In the past, most people would take guide books with **them** when **they** were travelling on holiday. But now, a combination of location apps on phones, information via Twitter and travel blogs has made **them** unnecessary. Information via **these** sources is more up to date and is often more useful because **it** is based on people's personal experience.

2 Link the pairs of sentences using a cause or result word or phrase.

1 Children are learning to use computers at school.
Many young people are better at computers than their parents.
2 Many people have a password to open programs on their computers.
They don't want other people to see their data.
3 Receiving spam can cause problems.
People install anti-spam programs.
4 Most businesses want their employees to be able to use computers.
There has been an increase in the number of computer courses available.
5 Computer chips are smaller and more powerful than ever before.
Computers can be smaller but faster.

3 Match note-making symbols 1–12 with meanings a–l.

1 ☐	∴	a	and
2 ☐	∵	b	greater than
3 ☐	=	c	falling/decreasing/dropping
4 ☐	≠	d	therefore/so
5 ☐	→	e	about/circa/c.
6 ☐	>	f	uncertain/not sure
7 ☐	<	g	does not equal/is not the same as
8 ☐	≅	h	equals/is the same as
9 ☐	↑	i	less than
10 ☐	↓	j	leads to/implies
11 ☐	&	k	because/as/since
12 ☐	?	l	rising/increasing/growing

9 Inventions, discoveries, and processes

READING SKILLS Intensive reading • Linking ideas (4)
WRITING SKILLS The passive voice • Clarifying a sequence • Writing a description of a process
RESEARCH Using indexes

READING How things work

1 Work with a partner. Read the sentences describing the benefits of five inventions. What inventions do they refer to?

  1 The sound quality is good and you can move freely as you speak.
  2 Connect to the Internet without plugging it into a phone line.
  3 You don't have to get out of the car – just press a button and drive in.
  4 You can listen for the baby crying from a different room.
  5 Use this to download music and take it with you wherever you go.

2 What makes the inventions work? Skim the title and paragraph 1 of the text on page 53 to check. Were you right?

3 **Read STUDY SKILL** Read paragraph 2 of the text. Answer the questions.

STUDY SKILL Intensive reading

Students often read intensively in order to make notes, or fully understand what they are reading.

To focus on the detail of what you are reading:

- ask yourself *why* you are reading and *what* you need from your reading. Skim the text including the title and any diagrams or tables, to get an overview.
- read the material from beginning to end. Circle words and phrases you don't know, but *don't* stop reading to look them up.
- read the material more slowly and underline/highlight the *main ideas*. Then make notes (see Study Skill p34) – if the text is very difficult, read it two or three more times before making notes.
- go back to the *new vocabulary* you circled. If necessary, look up the words in a dictionary. Record them appropriately (see Study Skill p8).

---

  1 What makes the 'voice waves' stronger?
  2 What sends out the 'radio waves'?
  3 What picks up the 'radio waves'?
  4 What are the 'radio waves' turned back into at first?

4 Find the words in the box in paragraph 2 and underline them. If necessary, check the meanings in a dictionary.

  | amplifier (x2)   headphones   large aerials |
  | radio waves (x2)   receiving aerials   voice waves (x2) |

5 Look at the diagram in the text. What does it show?

6 Read the text again. Label the diagram using the words from exercise 4. Compare your labelled diagram with a partner's.

The old-fashioned secret behind modern technology

1 Have you heard of Guglielmo Marconi? He is said to have invented radio at the end of the nineteenth century. Until television became widespread, radio was one of the basic means of communication and entertainment. The simple transistor radio may seem a little old-fashioned in these days of mobile phones, laptop computers, and iPods. However, radio waves, which are invisible and undetectable to humans, have changed the world completely. When you use a mobile or cordless phone, a wireless network for your laptop, or switch TV channels by remote control, you are using radio waves.

2 So, how does it work? Let's take a radio programme as an example. Firstly, in the studio the voices and music are turned into electronic signals, called 'voice waves'. Next, they are made stronger by passing them through an amplifier. These stronger waves are called 'carrier waves' and they are passed to large aerials. Then the aerials send out these waves, which are now called 'radio waves'. These are subsequently picked up by a receiving aerial, in this case, the one on your radio. After this, the radio waves go through a reverse process. They are first turned back into voice waves, then passed through another amplifier, and finally sent out through speakers or headphones. The result is your favourite music or the latest news!

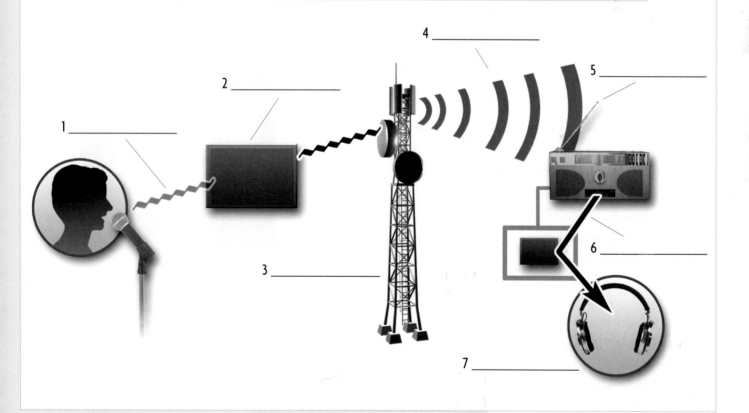

7 **Read STUDY SKILL** Look again at paragraph 2 of the text and underline eight sequencing words or expressions.

STUDY SKILL Linking ideas (4)

Sequencing words are used to link steps in a description of a process.

Some examples are:

- *Firstly, ... Secondly, ...* etc.
- *Then ... Next, ... After that, ... Subsequently, ...* etc.
- *Finally, ... Lastly, ...*

WRITING How things are made

1 **Read STUDY SKILL** Complete the sentences using the verb in brackets in the correct form of the passive.

STUDY SKILL The passive voice

When describing a process or a scientific experiment, it is important to write in a neutral style, as an observer.

To do this, you can use the passive voice.

The Present Simple Passive is often used in descriptions of processes:	The Past Simple Passive is often used to talk about inventions and discoveries:
is/are + past participle	*was/were* + past participle
Voices **are turned into** voice waves.	Radio **was invented by** Guglielmo Marconi.

---

1 The telephone _____ (invent) by Alexander Graham Bell.

2 A man _____ (send) into space for the first time in 1961.

3 X-rays _____ (discover) by William Roentgen.

4 Penicillin_____ first _____ (manufacture) in the 1940s.

5 Paper _____ (make) from trees.

6 A lot of paper _____ (recycle) these days.

7 Water and fats _____ (use) to make soap.

8 Glass _____ (make) from silica and limestone.

2 Read about the glass-making process. Complete the text with the verbs in brackets in the passive.

Glass was probably first made by the Egyptians about 5,000 years ago. It ¹_____(make) from silica, which comes from sand, limestone, and soda ash. Firstly, old glass ²_____(add) to the silica. Then, the silica and the old glass ³_____(mix) in a machine. Next, this mixture ⁴_____ (melt) in a furnace. Finally, the mixture ⁵_____ (press) into shapes such as light bulbs.

3 Read the notes about the soap-making process. Expand them into full sentences using the verbs in brackets in the passive.

1 hot water & oil/fat (mix together) *Hot water and oil and fat are mixed together.*

2 mixture (distil)

3 alkali & perfume (add, mix well)

4 mixture (roll, dry, compress)

5 soap (cut, wrap, pack)

Writing a description of a process

4 **Read STUDY SKILL** Write your sentences about the soap-making process into a paragraph. Use linking words from the box.

Firstly,	Next,	Then	After that,	Finally,

STUDY SKILL Clarifying a sequence

To describe a process clearly:
- divide the process into steps.
- make notes on each step.
- expand your notes into full sentences using the passive form.
- mark each step by using sequencing words.

RESEARCH Reference books

1 [Read STUDY SKILL] You want to find information from a reference book on subjects 1–12. Highlight or underline the word or category word. Compare answers with a partner.

1 Daniel Defoe
2 the Eiffel Tower
3 the South American country, Ecuador
4 deoxyribose nucleic acid
5 the Earth's atmosphere
6 the Sahara Desert
7 the Dead Sea
8 total eclipses of the sun
9 extinct animals, such as dinosaurs and dodos
10 how the diesel engine works
11 how long the river Danube is
12 Durban, South Africa

> **STUDY SKILL** Using indexes
>
> To use an index in a reference book:
> - decide which is the *keyword* and look for that, e.g. *the River Danube* (Danube), or what *category* the word might be in, e.g. *Gobi Desert* (Desert) and search for that.
> - scan alphabetically.
>
> If you can't find the reference, search again using another word in the phrase or title.

2 Look at the encyclopaedia index on page 56. Quickly find the page number for the information in exercise 1. Time yourself. Check your list and compare your time with a partner.

3 Where in the index would you add words 1–8?

1 Ecology   *between Eclipse and Economics*   5 Diet
2 Dynamite   6 Egg
3 Drum   7 Dragon
4 Dominica   8 Elephant

4 Look at the inventions a–h. Where necessary, underline the key word. When were they invented? Use a reference book or search engine to find out (see Study Skill p42).

5 Which two inventions are the most important and why? Discuss with a partner.

c flight

d the wheel

a the television

b the telephone

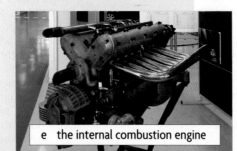
e the internal combustion engine

f the microwave oven

g the computer

h the steam engine

Dd

Ee

REVIEW Word-building (3)

1 ▪ Read STUDY SKILL ▪ Review the text on page 53 to complete the compound nouns.

1 _____ radio

2 _____ computer

3 _____ waves

4 voice _____

5 _____ programme

Review the text on page 53 to complete the compound nouns.

STUDY SKILL Compound nouns

A compound noun can be formed by putting two nouns together. Sometimes these are written:

▪ as two words, e.g. *radio waves*

▪ as one word, e.g. *microwave*

▪ with a hyphen, e.g. *data-processing*

Use a dictionary to check how to write them.

2 Match the nouns to form compound nouns. There may be more than one possible combination. Use a dictionary to find out how to write them.

1 ☐ information   a dish
2 ☐ DVD   b laboratory
3 ☐ answer   c machine
4 ☐ fax   d phone
5 ☐ word   e player
6 ☐ computer   f processor
7 ☐ satellite   g technology
8 ☐ physics   h virus

3 ▪ Read STUDY SKILL ▪ Complete the sentences. Use a compound adjective from the box.

STUDY SKILL Compound adjectives

A compound adjective can be made with:

▪ a noun + adjective, e.g. *computer literate*

▪ an adjective + present/past participle, e.g. *easy-going*

▪ an adverb + present/past participle, e.g. *well-known*

▪ an adjective + noun, e.g. *blue-eyed*

Use a dictionary to check how to write them.

hard-working	poorly-written
long-term	small-scale
self-motivated	high-speed
well-written	remote-controlled
highly-qualified	voice-powered

1 The new professor is a _____ biochemist.

2 Many devices around the house, such as televisions and CD players, are _____ .

3 Soon many home devices will use _____ technology, so you can tell them what to do!

4 Most science students do some _____ research at university.

5 _____ essays often get a few more marks than _____ ones.

6 Many countries are developing _____ trains as part of their public transport infrastructure.

7 Although most medicines do a lot of good, some have _____ side-effects.

8 Interviewers often look for students who are _____ as well as _____ .

4 Use your dictionary. Find other compound adjectives which begin *self-* , *highly-* , *well-* .

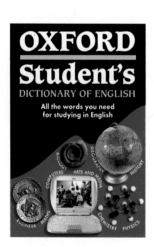

10 Travel and tourism

READING International tourism

1 Work with a partner. Discuss the questions.

1 When do most visitors come to your country?
2 Where do most visitors to your country come from?
3 What is the most popular destination for visitors?
4 Where do you go for *your* holidays?

2 Skim the graph, bar chart, and text on page 59. Are the sentences true (**T**) or false (**F**)? Correct the false sentences.

1 Paragraph 1 of the text describes the bar chart.
2 Paragraph 2 of the text talks about tourist destinations.
3 The graph shows the number of international tourists in 2009.
4 The bar chart shows the top twelve tourist destinations in the world.
5 Both diagrams show numbers in millions.

Turkey

3 Complete the text *International Tourism* using information from the graph and chart. **Read STUDY SKILL**

STUDY SKILL Interpreting data

Many scientific and academic texts contain statistics. These are often illustrated in graphs or charts.

Referring to graphs and charts while you are reading will help you to understand the text, and interpret the statistical data better.

- Skim the titles of the text and graphs and charts to get a general idea.
- Read the description of the horizontal and vertical data.
- Look at the graph or bar chart. Ask yourself questions:
    What is the general picture or trend?
    Are there any unexpected points?
- As you read the text, refer to the appropriate part of the diagram. Compare the information in the text with the information in the graphs and charts.

China

4 Discuss the questions with a partner.

1 Have you been to any of these ten places?
2 Which country or countries would you like to visit?

Italy

International tourism

Number of International Tourists 2009

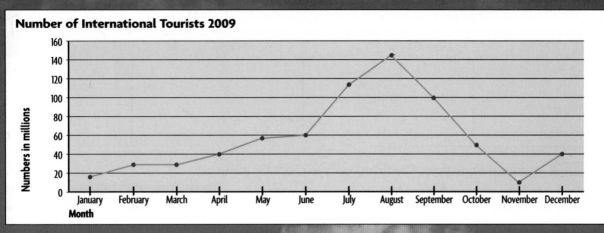

Tourist Destinations 2009

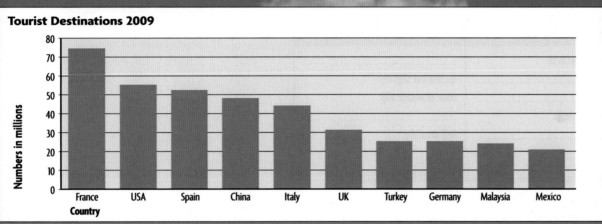

1 This graph shows the number of international [1]_____ , in millions, from January to December 2009.

At the start of the year, there were approximately [2]_____ international tourists. This number rose by 50% in [3]_____ to about 30 million. The number remained stable until March. Then it grew steadily to 40 million by April and this increase continued to the beginning of May. Between the beginning of May and the beginning of June, there was only a very slight increase, and then a dramatic rise in July and [4]_____ , reaching a peak of [5]_____ tourists around the world. Then in September it dropped suddenly to about 100 million, followed by a steady fall to the lowest point in [6]_____ . At the end of the year the number of tourists rose steadily to around 40 million.

Overall, the graph shows that the most popular period for international holidays is July and [7]_____ . The least popular time is [8]_____ and the beginning of the year, but there is a slight increase in [9]_____ .

2 The bar chart shows the top ten most popular international tourist destinations in 2009. The favourite holiday destination was [10]_____ , which about 74 million people visited in 2009. There was a drop of about 20 million to the second most liked holiday spot, the USA, with about 55 million visitors. In [11]_____ place was Spain, with around 52 million tourists a year. This was followed by [12]_____ , Italy, and the UK. There were fewer visitors to Turkey and [13]_____ , in seventh and eighth place respectively; only about [14]_____ million to each country. The ninth and tenth places were taken by Malaysia and Mexico. They received between [15]_____ and 24 million tourists each.

VOCABULARY DEVELOPMENT Varying vocabulary (2)

1 Write the words from the box in the table.

> fall   drop   rise   remain steady   increase   decrease
> fluctuate   remain stable   grow

go up ↑	go down ↓	go up and down ⤴	stay the same ⟶

2 Read STUDY SKILL Answer the questions. Use a dictionary to check the answers.

1 Which words are both verbs and nouns?
2 Which verbs are regular?

3 Look back at the text on page 59 to complete the table with phrases.

STUDY SKILL Avoiding repetition (3)

The language used to describe graphs can be repetitive. To avoid this, use:
- synonyms, e.g. *increase = rise*
- adjectives + nouns, e.g. *slight increase*
- verbs + adverbs, e.g. *increased slightly*

adjectives + nouns	verbs + adverbs
a steady growth	_____
_____	increased slightly
_____	rose dramatically
a sudden drop	_____
_____	fell steadily

4 Match an expression from exercise 3 with the graphs.

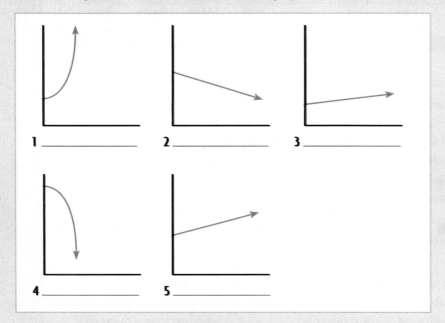

1 _____ 2 _____ 3 _____

4 _____ 5 _____

5 Complete the expressions with adjectives from exercise 3.

1 A _____ rise (or fall) is both large and fast.
2 A _____ growth (or drop) is small, slow, and regular.
3 A _____ increase (or decrease) is small.
4 A _____ drop (or rise) is fast and unexpected.

WRITING Graphs and bar charts

1 **Read STUDY SKILL** Work with a partner. Decide which way of illustrating data would be best for:

- showing the number of university students in a country from 2000 to 2010.
- showing the difference in the number of men at university and the number of women at university in 2006, 2008, and 2010.

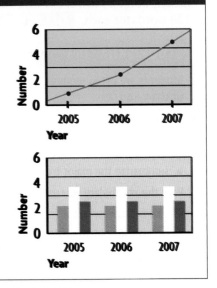
2 Look at the bar chart. Complete the text using the words in the box.

fewer	largest	more	same
smallest	than		

This bar chart shows the percentage of French, Russian, and Japanese tourists visiting my country.

In 1995 the ¹_____ percentage, 15%, of foreign visitors came from Russia. There were 5% ²_____ visitors from France and the ³_____ group (5%) were from Japan. This changed significantly in 2000, when there were ⁴_____ French visitors (12%) ⁵_____ Russians. Then, in 2005 there was a huge increase in the number of Japanese tourists, who formed the largest group (14%). The percentage of Russian and French visitors was the ⁶_____ , at 12%.

Overall, the percentage of French and Japanese visitors increased between 1995 and 2005, whereas the percentage of Russian tourists fell.

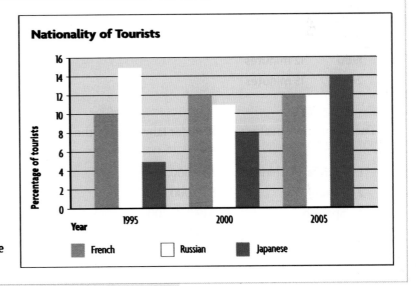

3 Look at the graph and complete the text with a suitable *noun, adjective, verb, adverb,* or *preposition.*

This graph shows the number of students at university ¹_____ 2000 and 2005.

In 2000 there were about 10,000 people studying at university. There was a slight ²_____ in 2001 to about 8,000. This was followed by a dramatic ³_____ to 22,000 ⁴_____ 2002. After this, the number ⁵_____ ⁶_____ at around 23,000 people for two years. Then, the number ⁷_____ ⁸_____ to approximately 32,000 by 2005.

Overall, the number of students continued to rise between 2000 and 2005, apart from a slight fall in 2001.

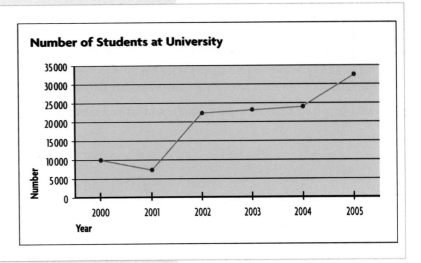

4 Draw a graph or a bar chart to illustrate the data in a and b. Write a description for each set of data and give the descriptions titles. Write about 120 words for each. `Read STUDY SKILL`

a The amount of time needed for an average worker to earn the money to buy 1 kilo of rice.

1900	75 minutes
1920	60 minutes
1940	35 minutes
1960	20 minutes
1980	12 minutes
2000	15 minutes

b The number of speakers of the major languages of the world.

1	Mandarin Chinese	845,000,000
2	Hindi	366,000,000
3	Spanish	329,000,000
4	English	328,000,000
5	Arabic	221,000,000
6	Bengali	181,000,000
7	Portuguese	178,000,000
8	Russian	144,000,000

Writing about data

5 Use the Internet or reference books to research one of the topics:
- the number of tourists to your country in the last three to five years.
- the number of men and women in your country in three different years.

Draw a graph or chart to show the data, and write a description.

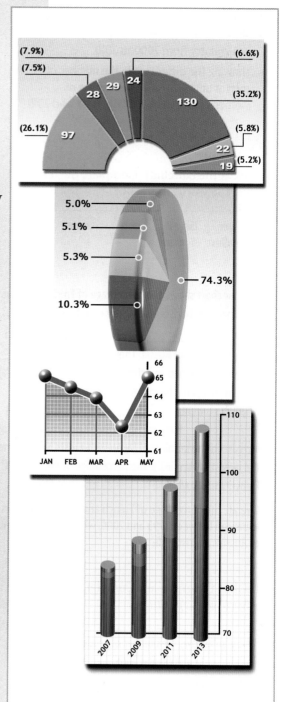

REVIEW

1 Read the description of a graph. Replace the words in bold with synonyms from the unit.

The graph shows the average cost of a one-week holiday for a family of four people from 1995 until 2005.

In 1995 the average cost of a holiday was $500. This **increased** dramatically in 1996 to $700 and then remained **stable** for the next year. However, in 1998 there was a slight **drop** to about $650. This was followed by a steady **rise** over the next two years to $800 by 2000. Between 2000 and 2003, the price **rose** dramatically again to $1,500. It remained steady at this level in 2004 and then there was **an increase** to a peak of $1,750 in 2005.

Overall, the graph shows that there has been a continual increase in the price of family holidays except for a slight **fall** in 1998.

2 Write a paragraph describing the graph.

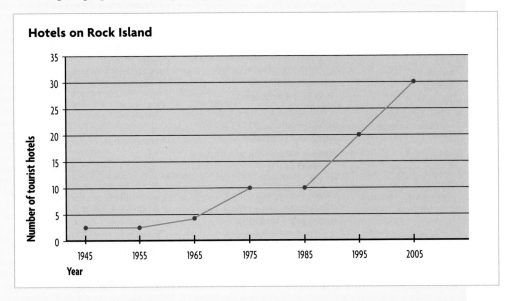

Hotels on Rock Island

3 Use the Internet or reference books to find out in which country/countries the languages are spoken.

Languages	Country/Countries
Mandarin Chinese	*China*
Hindi	
Spanish	
English	
Arabic	
Bengali	
Portuguese	
Russian	

WORD LIST

Here is a list of most of the new words in the units of *Headway Academic Skills* Level 2 Student's Book.

adj = adjective
adv = adverb
conj = conjunction
n = noun
pl = plural
prep = preposition
US = American English
v = verb

Unit 1

abroad *adv* /ə'brɔːd/
academic year *n* /ˌækədemɪk 'jɪə(r)/
accept *v* /ək'sept/
access *n* /'ækses/
accommodation *n* /əˌkɒmə'deɪʃn/
account number *n* /ə'kaʊnt ˌnʌmbə(r)/
advice *n* /əd'vaɪs/
application *n* /ˌæplɪ'keɪʃn/
application form *n* /ˌæplɪ'keɪʃn ˌfɔːm/
applied biochemistry *n* /əˌplaɪd ˌbaɪəʊ'kemɪstri/
apply for *v* /ə'plaɪ ˌfɔː(r), fə(r)/
arrival *n* /ə'raɪvl/
article (in a newspaper etc.) *n* /'ɑːtɪkl/
associated words *n pl* /ə'səʊsieɪtɪd ˌwɜːdz/
attitude *n* /'ætɪtjuːd/
available *adj* /ə'veɪləbl/
bank statement *n* /'bæŋk ˌsteɪtmənt/
basketball *n* /'bɑːskɪtbɔːl/
biography *n* /baɪ'ɒgrəfi/
birth certificate *n* /'bɜːθ səˌtɪfɪkət/
block capitals *n pl* /ˌblɒk 'kæpɪtlz/
boxes (on a form) *n pl* /'bɒksɪz/
brainstorm *v* /'breɪnstɔːm/
business *n* /'bɪznəs/
certificate *n* /sə'tɪfɪkət/
commence *v* /kə'mens/
complete *v* /kəm'pliːt/
concentrate *v* /'kɒnsəntreɪt/
credit card *n* /'kredɪt ˌkɑːd/
date of birth *n* /ˌdeɪt əv 'bɜːθ/
definition *n* /ˌdefɪ'nɪʃn/
delete as appropriate *v* /dɪˌliːt əz ə'prəʊpriət/
departure *n* /dɪ'pɑːtʃə(r)/
details *n pl* /'diːteɪlz/

dictionary entry *n* /'dɪkʃnri ˌentri/
document *n* /'dɒkjəmənt/
driving licence *n* /'draɪvɪŋ ˌlaɪsəns/
duration *n* /djʊ'reɪʃn/
effective *adj* /ɪ'fektɪv/
efficient *adj* /ɪ'fɪʃnt/
enjoyment *n* /ɪn'dʒɔɪmənt/
essential *adj* /ɪ'senʃl/
expiry date *n* /ɪk'spaɪəri ˌdeɪt/
extensive reading *n* /ɪkˌstensɪv 'riːdɪŋ/
female *adj* /'fiːmeɪl/
file (on a computer) *n* /faɪl/
final exams *n pl* /ˌfaɪnl ɪg'zæmz/
for future reference /fə ˌfjuːtʃə 'refrəns/
form *n* /fɔːm/
grades *n* /greɪdz/
hall of residence *n* /ˌhɔːl əv 'rezɪdəns/
handout *n* /'hændaʊt/
helpful *adj* /'helpfl/
highlight *v* /'haɪlaɪt/
homework *n* /'həʊmwɜːk/
host family *n* /ˌhəʊst 'fæməli/
ID *n* /ˌaɪ 'diː/
identify *v* /aɪ'dentɪfaɪ/
important *adj* /ɪm'pɔːtənt/
improve *v* /ɪm'pruːv/
indexes *n pl* /'ɪndeksɪz, 'ɪndɪsiːz/
informal letter *n* /ɪnˌfɔːml 'letə(r)/
information *n* /ˌɪnfə'meɪʃn/
ink *n* /ɪŋk/
instead *adv* /ɪn'sted/
instruction manuals *n pl* /ɪn'strʌkʃn ˌmænjʊəlz/
intensive reading *n* /ɪnˌtensɪv 'riːdɪŋ/
issue date *n* /'ɪʃuː ˌdeɪt/
journal *n* /'dʒɜːnl/
keep a record of *v* /ˌkiːp ə 'rekɔːd əv/
keyboard *n* /'kiːbɔːd/
literature *n* /'lɪtrətʃə(r)/
looking forward to *v* /'lʊkɪŋ ˌfɔːwəd tə/
main points *n pl* /'meɪn ˌpɔɪnts/
make the best of *v* /ˌmeɪk ðə 'best əv/
make notes *v* /ˌmeɪk 'nəʊts/
male *adj* /meɪl/
marital status *n* /'mærɪtl ˌsteɪtəs/
Master's Degree *n* /'mɑːstəz dɪˌgriː/
mention *v* /'menʃn/
method *n* /'meθəd/
middle name *n* /'mɪdl ˌneɪm/
mixture *n* /'mɪkstʃə(r)/

Miss /mɪs/
mobile telephone *n* /ˌməʊbaɪl 'telɪfəʊn/
Mr /'mɪstə(r)/
Mrs /'mɪsɪz/
Ms /məz/
MSc *n* /ˌem es 'siː/
nationality *n* /ˌnæʃə'næləti/
note *v* /nəʊt/
notebook *n* /'nəʊtbʊk/
novels *n pl* /'nɒvlz/
offer *n* /'ɒfə(r)/
official *adj* /ə'fɪʃl/
of interest *adj* /əv 'ɪntrəst/
particular *adj* /pə'tɪkjələ(r)/
particularly *adv* /pə'tɪkjələli/
passport *n* /'pɑːspɔːt/
plays *n pl* /pleɪz/
pleasure *n* /'pleʒə(r)/
poetry *n* /'pəʊətri/
postcode *n* /'pəʊstkəʊd/
prepare (for) *v* /prɪ'peə ˌfɔː(r), fə(r)/
print *v* /prɪnt/
process *n* /'prəʊses/
pronunciation *n* /prəˌnʌnsi'eɪʃn/
punctuation *n* /ˌpʌŋktʃu'eɪʃn/
purely *adv* /'pjʊəli/
reading materials *n pl* /'riːdɪŋ məˌtɪəriəlz/
reason *n* /'riːzn/
record (vocabulary) *v* /rɪ'kɔːd/
relevant *adj* /'reləvənt/
rented *adj* /'rentɪd/
reports *n pl* /rɪ'pɔːts/
required *adj* /rɪ'kwaɪəd/
research *n* /rɪ'sɜːtʃ, 'riːsɜːtʃ/
results *n pl* /rɪ'zʌlts/
ring *v* /rɪŋ/
scan *v* /skæn/
scanning *n* /'skænɪŋ/
scientific *adj* /ˌsaɪən'tɪfɪk/
search engine finds *n pl* /'sɜːtʃ ˌendʒɪn ˌfaɪndz/
set text *n* /ˌset 'tekst/
shared house *n* /ˌʃeəd 'haʊs/
single *adj* /'sɪŋgl/
skim *v* /skɪm/
skim reading *n* /'skɪm ˌriːdɪŋ/
soon *adv* /suːn/
special diet *n* /ˌspeʃl 'daɪət/
specify *v* /'spesɪfaɪ/
speed *n* /spiːd/
spellchecker *n* /'speltʃekə(r)/
spelling *n* /'spelɪŋ/
sports centre *n* /'spɔːts ˌsentə(r)/
statistic *n* /stə'tɪstɪk/
stress *n* /stres/
stressed syllables *n pl* /ˌstrest 'sɪləblz/
stress mark *n* /'stres ˌmɑːk/
stress pattern *n* /'stres ˌpætn/

study *n, v* /'stʌdi/
summarize *v* /'sʌməraɪz/
swimming pool *n* /'swɪmɪŋ ˌpuːl/
take your time *v* /ˌteɪk jɔː 'taɪm/
technology *n* /tek'nɒlədʒi/
telephone number *n* /'telɪfəʊn ˌnʌmbə(r)/
textbooks *n pl* /'tekstbʊks/
timetable *n* /'taɪmteɪbl/
time yourself *v* /'taɪm jəˌself/
title (person) *n* /'taɪtl/
tourism *n* /'tʊərɪzm/
translation *n* /træns'leɪʃn/
transport *n* /'trænspɔːt/
type *n* /taɪp/
university *n* /ˌjuːnɪ'vɜːsəti/
vegetarian *adj* /ˌvedʒɪ'teəriən/
vocabulary *n* /vəʊ'kæbjələri/
wherever *adv* /weər'evə(r)/
wireless connections *n pl* /ˌwaɪələs kə'nekʃnz/
wish *v* /wɪʃ/
word card *n* /'wɜːd ˌkɑːd/

Unit 2

aeroplane *n* /'eərəpleɪn/
Africa *n* /'æfrɪkə/
Algeria *n* /æl'dʒɪəriə/
although *conj* /ɔːl'ðəʊ/
amazing *adj* /ə'meɪzɪŋ/
Amazon *n* /'æməzən/
ancient *adj* /'eɪnʃnt/
antonyms *n pl* /'æntənɪmz/
apartment block *n* /ə'pɑːtmənt ˌblɒk/
Arab *adj* /'ærəb/
Arabic *n* /'ærəbɪk/
Asia *n* /'eɪʒə/
Atlantic Ocean *n* /ətˌlæntɪk 'əʊʃn/
attractions *n pl* /ə'trækʃnz/
Australia *n* /ɒ'streɪliə/
beaches *n pl* /'biːtʃɪz/
border *n, v* /'bɔːdə(r)/
business *n* /'bɪznəs/
capital *n* /'kæpɪtl/
castle *n* /'kɑːsl/
century *n* /'sentʃəri/
city-state *n* /'sɪti ˌsteɪt/
climb *v* /klaɪm/
coal *n* /kəʊl/
coastline *n* /'kəʊstlaɪn/
continents *n pl* /'kɒntɪnənts/
cottage *n* /'kɒtɪdʒ/
create *v* /kri'eɪt/
creation *n* /kri'eɪʃn/
depend on *v* /dɪ'pend ˌɒn/
desert *n* /'dezət/
destination *n* /ˌdestɪ'neɪʃn/
develop *v* /dɪ'veləp/

diagram *n* /'daɪəgræm/
differences *n pl* /'dɪfrənsɪz/
discard *v* /dɪs'kɑːd/

east *n, adj, adv* /iːst/
economy *n* /ɪ'kɒnəmi/
Eiffel Tower *n* /'aɪfl 'taʊə(r)/
Equator *n* /ɪ'kweɪtə(r)/
Euro Disney *n* /'jʊərə 'dɪzni/
Europe *n* /'jʊərəp/
fabulous *adj* /'fæbjələs/
famous *adj* /'feɪməs/
farming *n* /'fɑːmɪŋ/
France *n* /frɑːns/
fresh water *n* /,freʃ 'wɔːtə(r)/
frontier *n* /'frʌntɪə(r)/

gas *n* /gæs/
geography *n* /dʒi'ɒgrəfi/
govern *v* /'gʌvn/

historic *adj* /hɪ'stɒrɪk/
history *n* /'hɪstri/
however *conj* /haʊ'evə(r)/
include *v* /ɪn'kluːd/
including *prep* /ɪn'kluːdɪŋ/
independent *adj* /,ɪndɪ'pendənt/
industries *n pl* /'ɪndəstriz/
Irish Sea *n* /,aɪrɪʃ 'siː/
island *n* /'aɪlənd/

kingdom *n* /'kɪŋdəm/
km *n* /,keɪ 'em/

lake *n* /leɪk/
logically *adv* /'lɒdʒɪkli/
loud *adv* /laʊd/
Louvre *n* /'luːvrə/

Malay *n* /mə'leɪ/
Mandarin *n* /'mændərɪn/
man-made *adj* /,mæn 'meɪd/
manufacturing *n* /,mænjə'fæktʃərɪŋ/
Mediterranean Sea *n* /,medɪtə,reɪniən 'siː/
mining *n* /'maɪnɪŋ/
modern *adj* /'mɒdn/
Morocco *n* /mə'rɒkəʊ/
mountain *n* /'maʊntən/
mountain ranges *n pl* /'maʊntən ,reɪndʒɪz/
Mount Everest *n* /,maʊnt 'evərɪst/
museum *n* /mju'ziːəm/

national assembly *n* /,næʃnəl ə'sembli/
natural resources *n pl* /,nætʃrəl rɪ'zɔːsɪz/
Nile *n* /naɪl/
noisy *adj* /'nɔɪzi/
north *n, adj, adv* /nɔːθ/
northern *adj* /'nɔːðən/
North Pole *n* /,nɔːθ 'pəʊl/

ocean *n* /'əʊʃn/
official language *n* /ə,fɪʃl 'læŋgwɪdʒ/
oil *n* /ɔɪl/

polluted *adj* /pə'luːtɪd/
pond *n* /pɒnd/
popular *adj* /'pɒpjələ(r)/
rainforests *n pl* /'reɪnfɒrɪsts/

relax *v* /rɪ'læks/
republic *n* /rɪ'pʌblɪk/
revolution *n* /revə'luːʃn/
rule *v* /ruːl/

Sahara *n* /sə'hɑːrə/
scale *n* /skeɪl/
seashore *n* /'siːʃɔː(r)/
similarities *n pl* /,sɪmə'lærətiz/
Singapore *n* /,sɪŋə'pɔː(r)/
skiing *n* /ski:ŋ/
skyscraper *n* /'skaɪskreɪpə(r)/
south *n, adj, adv* /saʊθ/
South America *n* /,saʊθ ə'merɪkə/
south-east *adj* /,saʊθ 'iːst/
South Pole *n* /,saʊθ 'pəʊl/
space rocket *n* /'speɪs ,rɒkɪt/
synonyms *n pl* /'sɪnənɪmz/

Tamil *n* /'tæml/
topic areas *n pl* /'tɒpɪk ,eəriəz/
tourism *n* /'tʊərɪzm/
tourist *n* /'tʊərɪst/
traditional *adj* /trə'dɪʃənl/
United Kingdom *n* /jə,naɪtɪd 'kɪŋdəm/
unpolluted *adj* /,ʌnpə'luːtɪd/

Wales *n* /weɪlz/
Welsh *n* /welʃ/
west *n, adj, adv* /west/
western *adj* /'westən/
wild *adj* /waɪld/
world-famous *adj* /,wɜːld 'feɪməs/

zoo *n* /zuː/

Unit 3

airline *n* /'eəlaɪn/
apologize *v* /ə'pɒlədʒaɪz/
appropriate *adj* /ə'prəʊpriət/
at the top of his voice /ət ðə ,tɒp əv hɪz 'vɔɪs/
Australian *adj* /ɒ'streɪliən/

baggage *n* /'bægɪdʒ/
baggage handler *n* /'bægɪdʒ ,hændlə(r)/
baggage truck *n* /'bægɪdʒ ,trʌk/
balloon *n* /bə'luːn/
bang *v* /bæŋ/
boss *n* /bɒs/
briefcase *n* /'briːfkeɪs/
businessman *n* /'bɪznəsmən/
business people *n pl* /'bɪznəs ,piːpl/
businesswoman *n* /'bɪznəswʊmən/

captain *n* /'kæptɪn/
case *n* /keɪs/
catch *v* /kætʃ/
ceiling *n* /'siːlɪŋ/
commerce *n* /'kɒmɜːs/
comprehension *n* /,kɒmprɪ'henʃn/
conference *n* /'kɒnfərəns/
conference centre *n* /'kɒnfərəns ,sentə(r)/

content *n* /'kɒntent/
corridor *n* /'kɒrɪdɔː(r)/
cowboy boots *n pl* /'kaʊbɔɪ ,buːts/
customs *n pl* /'kʌstəmz/

die *v* /daɪ/
direct *adj* /də'rekt, dɪ-, daɪ-/
discover *v* /dɪ'skʌvə(r)/

encourage *v* /ɪn'kʌrɪdʒ/
events *n pl* /ɪ'vents/
examine *v* /ɪg'zæmɪn/
exhausting *adj* /ɪg'zɔːstɪŋ/
expect *v* /ɪk'spekt/
expected *adj* /ɪk'spektɪd/
experienced *adj* /ɪk'spɪəriənst/
explain *v* /ɪk'spleɪn/

fall asleep *v* /,fɔːl ə'sliːp/
first-class *adj* /'fɜːst ,klɑːs/
flight *n* /flaɪt/
flight attendant *n* /'flaɪt ə,tendənt/
focus on *v* /'fəʊkəs ,ɒn/
fortunately *adv* /'fɔːtʃənətli/
freezing *adj* /'friːzɪŋ/
French *adj* /frentʃ/
frightened *adj* /'fraɪtnd/
fruitful *adj* /'fruːtfl/

go through (his notes) *v* /'gəʊ ,θruː/
greet *v* /griːt/
guess *n* /ges/

hall *n* /hɔːl/
headline *n* /'hedlaɪn/
hold *n* /həʊld/
horrified *adj* /'hɒrɪfaɪd/
horror *n* /'hɒrə(r)/
hugely *adv* /'hjuːdʒli/
hurt *adj* /hɜːt/

identify *v* /aɪ'dentɪfaɪ/
illegal *adj* /ɪ'liːgl/
illegible *adj* /ɪ'ledʒəbl/
illogical *adj* /ɪ'lɒdʒɪkl/
immature *adj* /,ɪmə'tʃʊə(r)/
immediately *adv* /ɪ'miːdiətli/
immigration control *n* /,ɪmɪ,greɪʃn kən'trəʊl/
immobile *adj* /ɪ'məʊbaɪl/
impatient *adj* /ɪm'peɪʃnt/
impersonal *adj* /ɪm'pɜːsənl/
impossible *adj* /ɪm'pɒsəbl/
inappropriate *adj* /ɪnə'prəʊpriət/
increased *adj* /'ɪŋkriːst/
indirect *adj* /,ɪndə'rekt, ,ɪndɪ-, ,ɪndaɪ-/
inexperienced *adj* /,ɪnɪk'spɪəriənst/
in fact /,ɪn 'fækt/
inform *v* /ɪn'fɔːm/
irrelevant *adj* /ɪ'reləvənt/
irresponsible *adj* /,ɪrɪ'spɒnsəbl/

jeans *n pl* /dʒiːnz/
joke *v* /dʒəʊk/

kangaroo *n* /,kæŋgə'ruː/

large *adj* /lɑːdʒ/
legal *adj* /'liːgl/
legible *adj* /'ledʒəbl/
Libyan *adj* /'lɪbiən/

linking words *n pl* /'lɪŋkɪŋ ,wɜːdz/
load *v* /ləʊd/
logical *adj* /'lɒdʒɪkl/
look up *v* /'lʊk ,ʌp/
luckily *adv* /'lʌkəli/
lucky *adj* /'lʌki/

make sense *v* /,meɪk 'sens/
managing director *n* /,mænədʒɪŋ də'rektə(r), dɪ-, daɪ-/
mature *adj* /mə'tʃʊə(r)/
maximum *adj* /'mæksɪməm/
MD *n* /,em 'diː/
meeting *n* /'miːtɪŋ/
Middle East *n* /,mɪdl 'iːst/
minimum *adj* /'mɪnɪməm/
mistake *v* /mɪ'steɪk/
mistaken identity *n* /mɪ,steɪkn aɪ'dentəti/
mobile *adj* /'məʊbaɪl/
moment *n* /'məʊmənt/
moon *n* /muːn/

negative *adj* /'negətɪv/
newspaper article *n* /'njuːspeɪpər ,ɑːtɪkl/
nod (your head) *v* /,nɒd (jɔː 'hed)/
notice *v* /'nəʊtɪs/

on the job *adv* /,ɒn ðə 'dʒɒb/
on time *adv* /,ɒn 'taɪm/
organizer *n* /'ɔːgənaɪzə(r)/
overjoyed *adj* /,əʊvə'dʒɔɪd/

panic *v* /'pænɪk/
part-time *adj* /,pɑːt 'taɪm/
passenger *n* /'pæsɪndʒə(r)/
patient *adj* /'peɪʃnt/
petrified *adj* /'petrɪfaɪd/
pick (him) up *v* /,pɪk ... 'ʌp/
pilot *n* /'paɪlət/
place *v* /pleɪs/
plan *v* /plæn/
positive *adj* /'pɒzətɪv/
possibilities *n pl* /,pɒsə'bɪlətiz/
possible *adj* /'pɒsəbl/
predict *v* /prə'dɪkt/
prefix *n* /'priːfɪks/
prepared to *adj* /prɪ'peəd tə/
presentations *n pl* /,prezən'teɪʃnz/
private *adj* /'praɪvət/
promise *v* /'prɒmɪs/
public *adj* /'pʌblɪk/
pump *v* /pʌmp/
punctuate *v* /'pʌŋktʃueɪt/
put right *v* /,pʊt 'raɪt/

regular *adj* /'regjələ(r)/
relations *n pl* /rɪ'leɪʃnz/
relatives *n pl* /'relətɪvz/
relevant *adj* /'reləvənt/
relief *n* /rɪ'liːf/
reply *v* /rɪ'plaɪ/
reporters *n pl* /rɪ'pɔːtəz/
responsible *adj* /rɪ'spɒnsəbl/
rest *n* /rest/
return ticket *n* /rɪ'tɜːn ,tɪkɪt/
rush *v* /rʌʃ/

Scottish *adj* /'skɒtɪʃ/
seminar *n* /'semɪnɑː(r)/

shift *n* /ʃɪft/
sign *n* /saɪn/
situation *n* /ˌsɪtʃʊ'eɪʃn/
smartly-dressed *adj* /ˌsmɑːtli 'drest/
smartly-suited *adj* /'smɑːtli ˌsuːtɪd/
solve *v* /sɒlv/
speech *n* /spiːtʃ/
speed *v* /spiːd/
spread *v* /spred/
stare *v* /steə(r)/
stay *n* /steɪ/
stowaway *n* /'stəʊəweɪ/
successful *adj* /sək'sesfl/
suitcases *n pl* /'suːtkeɪsɪz/
survive *v* /sə'vaɪv/
systems *n pl* /'sɪstəmz/
talk *n* /tɔːk/
terrible *adj* /'terəbl/
therefore *conj* /'ðeəfɔː(r)/
top *adj* /tɒp/
trade *n* /treɪd/
travel *v* /'trævl/
uncomfortable *adj* /ˌʌn'kʌmftəbl/
unexpected *adj* /ˌʌnɪk'spektɪd/
unfortunately *adv* /ˌʌn'fɔːtʃənətli/
unhurt *adj* /ˌʌn'hɜːt/
unknown *adj* /ˌʌn'nəʊn/
variety *n* /və'raɪəti/
violin *n* /ˌvaɪə'lɪn/

Unit 4

accelerate *v* /ək'seləreɪt/
accelerator *n* /ək'seləreɪtə(r)/
according to *prep* /ə'kɔːdɪŋ tə/
achieve *v* /ə'tʃiːv/
acoustic *adj* /ə'kuːstɪk/
advantages *n pl* /əd'vɑːntɪdʒɪz/
aim *n* /eɪm/
aircraft *n* /'eəkrɑːft/
amount *n* /ə'maʊnt/
announce *v* /ə'naʊns/
anytime *adv* /'enitaɪm/
at all times /ət ˌɔːl 'taɪmz/
automobile *n US* /'ɔːtəməˌbiːl/
ban *v* /bæn/
basic *adj* /'beɪsɪk/
benefit *v* /'benəfɪt/
brakes *n pl* /breɪks/
brilliant *adj* /'brɪliənt/
cause *v* /kɔːz/
channel *n* /'tʃænl/
choice *n* /tʃɔɪs/
circuit *n* /'sɜːkɪt/
city-dwellers *n pl* /'sɪti ˌdweləz/
clutch *n* /klʌtʃ/
cockpit *n* /'kɒkpɪt/
computer games *n pl* /kəm'pjuːtə ˌgeɪmz/
conclusion *n* /kən'kluːʒn/
conditions *n pl* /kən'dɪʃnz/
constantly *adv* /'kɒnstəntli/
content *n* /'kɒntent/
control *v* /kən'trəʊl/

convenience *n* /kən'viːniəns/
copy *n* /'kɒpi/
correspondent *n* /ˌkɒrɪ'spɒndənt/
crash *v* /kræʃ/
credit cards *n pl* /'kredɪt ˌkɑːdz/
cultures *n pl* /'kʌltʃəz/
damage *v* /'dæmɪdʒ/
data *n* /'deɪtə/
dependent *adj* /dɪ'pendənt/
design *v* /dɪ'zaɪn/
despite *prep* /dɪ'spaɪt/
development *n* /dɪ'veləpmənt/
device *n* /dɪ'vaɪs/
digital camera *n* /ˌdɪdʒɪtl 'kæmərə/
directly *adv* /də'rektli, dɪ-, daɪ-/
disadvantages *n pl* /ˌdɪsəd'vɑːntɪdʒɪz/
disagree *v* /ˌdɪsə'griː/
disaster *n* /dɪ'zɑːstə(r)/
documentary *n* /ˌdɒkjə'mentri/
download *v* /ˌdaʊn'ləʊd/
drawbacks *n pl* /'drɔːbæks/
driverless *adj* /'draɪvələs/
edit *v* /'edɪt/
electronic *adj* /ɪˌlek'trɒnɪk/
emergency exit *n* /ɪ'mɜːdʒənsi ˌeksɪt/
engines *n pl* /'endʒɪnz/
essential *adj* /ɪ'senʃl/
everyday *adj* /'evrideɪ/
own *v* /əʊn/
fed up *adj* /ˌfed 'ʌp/
finally *adv* /'faɪnəli/
firstly *adv* /'fɜːstli/
for example /fər ɪg'zɑːmpl/
for instance /fər 'ɪnstəns/
free time *n* /ˌfriː 'taɪm/
furthermore *adv* /ˌfɜːðə'mɔː(r)/
future *n* /'fjuːtʃə(r)/
go wrong *v* /ˌgəʊ 'rɒŋ/
grow *v* /grəʊ/
guide *n* /gaɪd/
harm *n* /hɑːm/
heating *n* /'hiːtɪŋ/
hobbies *n pl* /'hɒbiz/
huge *adj* /hjuːdʒ/
ideal *adj* /aɪ'diːəl/
identify *v* /aɪ'dentɪfaɪ/
in addition /ˌɪn ə'dɪʃn/
in conclusion /ˌɪn kən'kluːʒn/
in contrast /ˌɪn 'kɒntrɑːst/
increase *n* /'ɪŋkriːs/
industry *n* /'ɪndəstri/
insist *v* /ɪn'sɪst/
install *v* /ɪn'stɔːl/
instead of *prep* /ɪn'sted əv/
in the first place /ˌɪn ðə 'fɜːst ˌpleɪs/
introduction *n* /ˌɪntrə'dʌkʃn/
irritating *adj* /'ɪrɪteɪtɪŋ/
keep in touch *v* /ˌkiːp ɪn 'tʌtʃ/
laptop *n* /'læptɒp/
lastly *adv* /'lɑːstli/
latest *adj* /'leɪtɪst/
leisure *n* /'leʒə(r)/
let (sb) know *v* /ˌlet ... 'nəʊ/

lighting *n* /'laɪtɪŋ/
magnetic *adj* /mæg'netɪk/
manage *v* /'mænɪdʒ/
manufacture *v* /ˌmænjə'fæktʃə(r)/
manufacturer *n* /ˌmænjə'fæktʃərə(r)/
material *n* /mə'tɪəriəl/
memory sticks *n pl* /'meməri ˌstɪks/
message *n* /'mesɪdʒ/
microprocessor *n* /ˌmaɪkrəʊ'prəʊsesə(r)/
mobile phone *n* /ˌməʊbaɪl 'fəʊn/
models *n pl* /'mɒdlz/
motorways *n pl* /'məʊtəweɪz/
movie *n* /'muːvi/
multi-billion *adj* /ˌmʌlti ˌbɪljən/
needs *n pl* /niːdz/
old-fashioned *adj* /ˌəʊld 'fæʃnd/
on the other hand /ˌɒn ði 'ʌðə ˌhænd/
opinion *n* /ə'pɪnjən/
opportunity *n* /ˌɒpə'tjuːnəti/
opposite *n* /'ɒpəzɪt/
order *v* /'ɔːdə(r)/
origins *n pl* /'ɒrɪdʒɪnz/
outlaw *v* /'aʊtlɔː/
outline *v* /'aʊtlaɪn/
ovens *n pl* /'ʌvnz/
overhead *adv* /ˌəʊvə'hed/
ownership *n* /'əʊnəʃɪp/
pass *v* /pɑːs/
phone call *n* /'fəʊn ˌkɔːl/
photographer *n* /fə'tɒgrəfə(r)/
pilot *n* /'paɪlət/
plans *n pl* /plænz/
preview *v* /'priːvjuː/
previous *adj* /'priːviəs/
professional *adj* /prə'feʃənl/
project *n* /'prɒdʒekt/
protect *v* /prə'tekt/
quality *n* /'kwɒləti/
radar *n* /'reɪdɑː(r)/
rear-view mirror *n* /ˌrɪə ˌvjuː 'mɪrə(r)/
receive *v* /rɪ'siːv/
reduce *v* /rɪ'djuːs/
reduction *n* /rɪ'dʌkʃn/
related to *adj* /rɪ'leɪtɪd ˌtuː, tə/
repetitive *adj* /rɪ'petətɪv/
require *v* /rɪ'kwaɪə(r)/
rise *v* /raɪz/
rude *adj* /ruːd/
satellite TV *n* /ˌsætəlaɪt ˌtiː 'viː/
save *v* /seɪv/
scan *v* /skæn/
scanners *n pl* /'skænəz/
secondly *adv* /'sekndli/
security *n* /sɪ'kjʊərəti/
select *v* /sɪ'lekt/
sensor *n* /'sensə(r)/
set up *v* /ˌset 'ʌp/
significant *adj* /sɪg'nɪfɪkənt/
silent *adj* /'saɪlənt/
SIM cards *n pl* /'sɪm ˌkɑːdz/
slow down *v* /ˌsləʊ 'daʊn/

smart cards *n pl* /'smɑːt ˌkɑːdz/
special *adj* /'speʃl/
speed up *v* /ˌspiːd 'ʌp/
steal *v* /stiːl/
steer *v* /stɪə(r)/
steering wheel *n* /'stɪərɪŋ ˌwiːl/
store *v* /stɔː(r)/
straight away *adv* /ˌstreɪt ə'weɪ/
street crime *n* /'striːt ˌkraɪm/
strongly *adv* /'strɒŋli/
suggest *v* /sə'dʒest/
suggestion *n* /sə'dʒestʃən/
support *v* /sə'pɔːt/
system *n* /'sɪstəm/
take off *v* /ˌteɪk 'ɒf/
topic sentences *n pl* /'tɒpɪk ˌsentənsɪz/
to conclude /tə kən'kluːd/
to sum up /tə ˌsʌm 'ʌp/
typewriter *n* /'taɪpraɪtə(r)/
tyres *n pl* /'taɪəz/
unreliable *adj* /ˌʌnrɪ'laɪəbl/
unsuitable *adj* /ˌʌn'suːtəbl/
use *n* /juːs/
value *n* /'væljuː/
vehicles *n pl* /'viːəklz/
voice-controlled *adj* /'vɔɪs kənˌtrəʊld/
waste *v* /weɪst/
what's more *adv* /ˌwɒts 'mɔː(r)/
white lines *n pl* /ˌwaɪt 'laɪnz/
wing *n* /wɪŋ/
within *prep* /wɪ'ðɪn/
wonderful *adj* /'wʌndəfl/
yours /jɔːz/
yours faithfully /ˌjɔːz 'feɪθfəli/

Unit 5

academic *adj* /ˌækə'demɪk/
acre *n* /'eɪkə(r)/
agriculture *n* /'ægrɪkʌltʃə(r)/
antiseptic *n* /ˌæntɪ'septɪk/
appear *v* /ə'pɪə(r)/
applicants *n pl* /'æplɪkənts/
arguments *n pl* /'ɑːgjəmənts/
arrange *v* /ə'reɪndʒ/
as requested /əz rɪ'kwestɪd/
attach *v* /ə'tætʃ/
attachment *n* /ə'tætʃmənt/
attend *v* /ə'tend/
audience *n* /'ɔːdiəns/
autobiography *n* /ˌɔːtəbaɪ'ɒgrəfi/
beauty *n* /'bjuːti/
Best wishes /ˌbest 'wɪʃɪz/
biannual *adj* /baɪ'ænjuəl/
bilingual *adj* /ˌbaɪ'lɪŋgwəl/
biochemistry *n* /ˌbaɪəʊ'kemɪstri/
biography *n* /baɪ'ɒgrəfi/
biological sciences *n pl* /ˌbaɪəˌlɒdʒɪkl 'saɪənsɪz/
book *v* /bʊk/
bower *n* /'baʊə(r)/
brief *adj* /briːf/
bursary *n* /'bɜːsəri/
candidates *n pl* /'kændɪdeɪts/

carbon *n* /'kɑ:bən/
chair *n, v* /ʧeə(r)/
characteristic *n* /,kærəktə'rɪstɪk/
check in *v* /,ʧek 'ɪn/
Cheers /ʧɪəz/
chemistry *n* /'kemɪstri/
chicken *n* /'ʧɪkɪn/
clear *adj* /klɪə(r)/
coach *n* /kəʊʧ/
coffee break *n* /'kɒfi ,breɪk/
colleagues *n pl* /'kɒli:gz/
collection *n* /kə'lekʃn/
conference *n* /'kɒnfərəns/
contact details *n pl* /'kɒntækt ,di:teɪlz/
contents *n pl* /'kɒntents/
cream *n* /'kri:m/
criticism *n* /'krɪtɪsɪzm/
currently *adv* /'kʌrəntli/
cut *n* /'kʌt/

depart *v* /dɪ'pɑ:t/
development *n* /dɪ'veləpmənt/
difficulty *n* /'dɪfɪkəlti/
dysphagia *n* /dɪs'feɪʤiə/

energetic *adj* /,enə'ʤetɪk/
essay *n* /'eseɪ/
exhibition *n* /,eksɪ'bɪʃn/
expert *n* /'ekspɜ:t/
ex-president *n* /,eks 'prezɪdənt/
familiar *adj* /fə'mɪliə(r)/
farewell *n* /,feə'wel/
farm *n* /fa:m/
fax *n* /fæks/
features *n pl* /'fi:ʧəz/
fields (academic) *n pl* /'fi:ldz/
final *adj* /'faɪnl/
fluently *adv* /'flu:əntli/
former *adj* /'fɔ:mə(r)/

gases *n pl* /'gæsɪz/
graduate *v* /'grædjʊeɪt/
great *adj* /greɪt/
gust *n* /gʌst/
head *n* /hed/
hedge *n* /heʤ/
hold (a conference) *v* /həʊld/
I'd love to… /,aɪd 'lʌv tə/
I have great pleasure in… /,aɪ hæv 'greɪt ,pleʒər ɪn/
I look forward to… /,aɪ 'lʊk ,fɔ:wəd tə/
improve *v* /ɪm'pru:v/
in charge /,ɪn 'ʧɑ:ʤ/
in favour of *prep* /,ɪn 'feɪvər əv/
infected *adj* /ɪn'fektɪd/
inflammatory *adj* /ɪn'flæmətri/
inform *v* /ɪn'fɔ:m/
informally *adv* /ɪn'fɔ:məli/
inherent *adj* /ɪn'herənt/
in support of /,ɪn sə'pɔ:t əv/
intermediate *adj* /,ɪntə'mi:diət/
international *adj* /,ɪntə'næʃnəl/
invitation *n* /,ɪnvɪ'teɪʃn/
itinerary *n* /aɪ'tɪnərəri/
It would be greatly appreciated if… /,ɪt wʊd bɪ 'greɪtli ə,pri:ʃieɪtɪd ɪf/
joy *n* /ʤɔɪ/

latter *adj* /'lætə(r)/
layout *n* /'leɪaʊt/
lesions *n pl* /'li:ʒnz/
liquid *n* /'lɪkwɪd/
literary *adj* /'lɪtərəri/
loveliness *n* /'lʌvlinəs/
malaria *n* /mə'leəriə/
medical *adj* /'medɪkl/
microphone *n* /'maɪkrəfəʊn/
ministry *n* /'mɪnəstri/
misprint *n* /'mɪsprɪnt/
mosque *n* /mɒsk/
multimedia *n* /,mʌltɪ'mi:diə/
national *adj* /'næʃnəl/
note *n* /nəʊt/
noted *adj* /'nəʊtɪd/
nothingness *n* /'nʌθɪŋnəs/
novel *n* /'nɒvl/
novelist *n* /'nɒvəlɪst/
nuclear power stations *n pl* /,nju:kliə 'paʊə ,steɪʃnz/
obstruction *n* /əb'strʌkʃn/
obvious *adj* /'ɒbviəs/
open air *n* /,əʊpən 'eə(r)/
overall *adj* /,əʊvər'ɔ:l/
paper (at a conference) *n* /'peɪpə(r)/
particularly *adv* /pə'tɪkjələli/
patient *n* /'peɪʃnt/
Please find attached … /'pli:z faɪnd ə,tæʧt/
Please find enclosed… /'pli:z faɪnd ɪn,kləʊzd/
plenary *n* /'pli:nəri/
poem *n* /'pəʊɪm/
poet *n* /'pəʊɪt/
point *v* /pɔɪnt/
postgraduate *n* /,pəʊst 'græʤʊət/
prefix *n* /'pri:fɪks/
printing *n* /'prɪntɪŋ/
prof. (professor) *n* /prɒf/
programme of events *n* /,prəʊgræm əv ɪ'vents/
prominent *adj* /'prɒmɪnənt/
purpose *n* /'pɜ:pəs/
qualifications *n pl* /,kwɒlɪfɪ'keɪʃnz/

reasonable *adj* /'ri:znəbl/
reduce *v* /rɪ'dju:s/
reference *n* /'refrəns/
remind *v* /rɪ'maɪnd/
reminder *n* /rɪ'maɪndə(r)/
renewable *adj* /rɪ'nju:əbl/
review *v* /rɪ'vju:/
screen *n* /skri:n/
senior lecturer *n* /,si:niə 'lekʧərə(r)/
session *n* /'seʃn/
set off *v* /,set 'ɒf/
shelter *n* /'ʃeltə(r)/
sightseeing *n* /'saɪtsi:ɪŋ/
site *n* /saɪt/
skills *n pl* /skɪlz/
social life *n* /'səʊʃl ,laɪf/
sources *n pl* /'sɔ:sɪz/
speaker *n* /'spi:kə(r)/

specify *v* /'spesɪfaɪ/
submarine *n* /,sʌbmə'ri:n/
suffixes *n pl* /'sʌfɪksɪz/
swallow *v* /'swɒləʊ/
symptom *n* /'sɪmptəm/
temporary *adj* /'tempərəri/
term (= word) *n* /tɜ:m/
textbook *n* /'tekstbʊk/
tone *n* /təʊn/
topography *n* /tə'pɒgrəfi/
tour *n* /tʊə(r)/
transform *v* /træns'fɔ:m/
translation *n* /træns'leɪʃn/
Turkey *n* /'tɜ:ki/
tutor *n* /'tju:tə(r)/
typical *adj* /'tɪpɪkl/
typing *n* /taɪpɪŋ/
use *n* /ju:s/
venue *n* /'venju:/
wedding *n* /'wedɪŋ/
wish *v* /wɪʃ/
Yours sincerely /,jɔ:z sɪn'sɪəli/

Unit 6

actually *adv* /'ækʧʊəli/
ancestors *n pl* /'ænsestəz/
ancient *adj* /'eɪnʃnt/
applied science *n* /ə,plaɪd 'saɪəns/
apply *v* /ə'plaɪ/
arthritis *n* /ɑ:'θraɪtəs/
asthma *n* /'æsmə/
author *n* /'ɔ:θə(r)/
average *adj* /'ævərɪʤ/
bestseller *n* /,best'selə(r)/
billion *n* /'bɪljən/
bones *n pl* /bəʊnz/
breakthrough *n* /'breɪkθru:/
bullet points *n pl* /'bʊlɪt ,pɔɪnts/
busy *adj* /'bɪzi/
bytes *n pl* /baɪts/
Canada *n* /'kænədə/
Canadian *adj* /kə'neɪdiən/
cause *n* /kɔ:z/
Celsius *n* /'selsiəs/
centigrade *n* /'sentɪgreɪd/
central *adj* /'sentrəl/
childhood *n* /'ʧaɪldhʊd/
chips *n pl* /ʧɪps/
claim *v* /kleɪm/
claims *n pl* /kleɪmz/
colleagues *n pl* /'kɒli:gz/
concentrate *v* /'kɒnsəntreɪt/
conclude *v* /kən'klu:d/
connection *n* /kə'nekʃn/
consist *v* /kən'sɪst/
contribute *v* /kən'trɪbju:t, 'kɒntrɪbju:t/
contributor *n* /kən'trɪbjətə(r)/
cures *n pl* /kjʊəz/
daily *adj* /'deɪli/
damage *n* /'dæmɪʤ/
danger *n* /'deɪnʤə(r)/
data *n* /'deɪtə/
decades *n pl* /'dekeɪdz/
decimals *n pl* /'desɪmlz/

decline *n* /dɪ'klaɪn/
decrease *v* /dɪ'kri:s/
demand *n* /dɪ'mɑ:nd/
depend *v* /dɪ'pend/
develop *v* /dɪ'veləp/
diameter *n* /daɪ'æmɪtə(r)/
diet *n* /'daɪət/
diseases *n pl* /dɪ'zi:zɪz/
distrust *n* /dɪs'trʌst/
drop *n* /drɒp/
effect *n* /ɪ'fekt/
elements *n pl* /'eləmənts/
ensure *v* /ɪn'ʃʊə(r)/
equals *v* /'i:kwəlz/
evidence *n* /'evɪdəns/
exist *v* /ɪg'zɪst/
face masks *n pl* /'feɪs ,mɑ:sks/
fact *n* /fækt/
factories *n pl* /'fæktəriz/
fight *v, n* /faɪt/
final *n* /'faɪnl/
forest fires *n pl* /'fɒrɪst ,faɪəz/
fossil fuels *n pl* /'fɒsl ,fjʊəlz/
generations *n pl* /,ʤenə'reɪʃnz/
gigabyte *n* /'gɪgəbaɪt/
habits *n pl* /'hæbɪts/
half *n* /hɑ:f/
heart attacks *n pl* /'hɑ:t ə,tæks/
height *n* /haɪt/
ill health *n* /,ɪl 'helθ/
increase *n* /'ɪŋkri:s/
increased *adj* /ɪŋ'kri:st/
increasing *adj* /ɪn'kri:sɪŋ/
increasingly *adv* /ɪn'kri:sɪŋli/
industrial *adj* /ɪn'dʌstriəl/
in fact *adv* /,ɪn 'fækt/
interpret *v* /ɪn'tɜ:prɪt/
in turn *adv* /,ɪn 'tɜ:n/
key *adj* /ki:/
latest *adj* /'leɪtɪst/
lead to *v* /'li:d ,tu:, tə/
less than /'les ðən/
level *n* /'levl/
likely *adj* /'laɪkli/
link *n* /lɪŋk/
long-term *adj* /,lɒŋ 'tɜ:m/
lung cancer *n* /'lʌŋ ,kænsə(r)/
major *adj* /'meɪʤə(r)/
make notes *v* /,meɪk 'nəʊts/
man-made *adj* /,mæn 'meɪd/
mathematical symbol *n* /,mæθə,mætɪkl 'sɪmbl/
metres *n pl* /'mi:təz/
microns *n pl* /'maɪkrɒnz/
mining *n* /'maɪnɪŋ/
minus *prep* /'maɪnəs/
motor vehicle *n* /'məʊtə ,vi:əkl/
natural *adj* /'næʧrəl/
nought *n* /nɔ:t/
oil *n* /ɔɪl/
ordinal numbers *n pl* /'ɔ:dɪnl ,nʌmbəz/
original *adj* /ə'rɪʤənl/
origins *n pl* /'ɒrɪʤɪnz/
paraphrase *v* /'pærəfreɪz/
particles *n pl* /'pɑ:tɪklz/

percentages n pl /pə'sentədʒɪz/
pi n /paɪ/
plagiarize v /'pleɪdʒəraɪz/
pollutants n pl /pə'lu:tənts/
polluted adj /pə'lu:tɪd/
pollution n /pə'lu:ʃn/
poorly adv /'pɔ:li, 'puəli/
possibility n /,pɒsə'bɪləti/
power stations n pl /'pauə
    ,steɪʃnz/
previously adv /'pri:viəsli/
primary school n /'praɪməri
    ,sku:l/
probably adv /'prɒbəbli/
prominent adj /'prɒmɪnənt/
properly adv /'prɒpəli/
protect v /prə'tekt/
prove v /pru:v/
pupils n pl /'pju:plz/
pure science n /,pjuə 'saɪəns/
quarter n /'kwɔ:tə(r)/
quote v /kwəut/
ratio n /'reɪʃiəu/
reaction n /ri'ækʃn/
reassuring adj /,ri:ə'ʃuərɪŋ/
record v /rɪ'kɔ:d/
reduce v /rɪ'dju:s/
relevant adj /'reləvənt/
report v /rɪ'pɔ:t/
researchers n pl /rɪ'sɜ:tʃəz/
residents n pl /'rezɪdənts/
result in v /rɪ'zʌlt ɪn/
results n pl /rɪ'zʌlts/
reveal v /rɪ'vi:l/
revision n /rɪ'vɪʒn/
rewrite v /,ri:'raɪt/
rise n /raɪz/
risk n /rɪsk/
sake n /seɪk/
scandal n /'skændl/
scientists n pl /'saɪəntɪsts/
search v /sɜ:tʃ/
shock v /ʃɒk/
shockingly adv /'ʃɒkɪŋli/
shortage n /'ʃɔ:tɪdʒ/
similar adj /'sɪmələ(r)/
single adj /'sɪŋgl/
sit (an exam) v /,sɪt (ən ɪg'zæm)/
skeletons n pl /'skelɪtnz/
society n /sə'saɪəti/
solution n /sə'lu:ʃn/
source n /sɔ:s/
speculate v /'spekjəleɪt/
speculation n /,spekjə'leɪʃn/
strictly adv /'strɪktli/
suburb n /'sʌbɜ:b/
suffer v /'sʌfə(r)/
summarize v /'sʌməraɪz/
summary n /'sʌməri/
take time v /,teɪk 'taɪm/
TB n /,ti: 'bi:/
temperature n /'temprətʃə(r)/
third n /θɜ:d/
three quarters n pl /,θri:
    'kwɔ:təz/
tiny adj /'taɪni/
toe n /təu/
tuberculosis n /tju:,bɜ:kju'ləusɪs/

uncertainty n /,ʌn'sɜ:tnti/
undervalue v /,ʌndə'vælju:/
unsurprisingly adv
    /,ʌnsə'praɪzɪŋli/
value n /'vælju:/
vehicle n /'vi:əkl/
vitamin C n /vɪtəmin'si:/
volcanoes n pl /vɒl'keɪnəuz/
zero n /'zɪərəu/

Unit 7

abstract n /'æbstrækt/
accompany v /ə'kʌmpəni/
actor n /'æktə(r)/
additional adj /ə'dɪʃənl/
admire v /əd'maɪə(r)/
age (= period of time) n /eɪdʒ/
Angola n /æŋ'gəulə/
annual adj /'ænjuəl/
apartheid n /ə'pɑ:taɪt/
approximately adv
    /ə'prɒksɪmətli/
Arabic adj /'ærəbɪk/
Arabism n /'ærəbɪzm/
archaeologist n /,ɑ:ki'ɒlədʒɪst/
Argentina n /,ɑ:dʒən'ti:nə/
art gallery n /'ɑ:t ,gæləri/
attend v /ə'tend/
author n /'ɔ:θə(r)/
average adj /'ævərɪdʒ/
best-selling adj /'best ,selɪŋ/
boiling point n /'bɔɪlɪŋ pɔɪnt/
bridge n /brɪdʒ/
butterfly n /'bʌtəflaɪ/
career n /kə'rɪə(r)/
categories n pl /'kætəgəriz/
century n /'sentʃəri/
chant v /tʃɑ:nt/
chart n /tʃɑ:t/
chemistry n /'kemɪstri/
chronological adj /,krɒnə'lɒdʒɪkl/
classic adj, n /'klæsɪk/
club n /klʌb/
collected adj /kə'lektɪd/
comedy n /'kɒmədi/
commas n pl /'kɒməz/
complete v /kəm'pli:t/
compose v /kəm'pəuz/
composer n /kəm'pəuzə(r)/
conditions n pl /kən'dɪʃnz/
conduct v /kən'dʌkt/
conductor n /kən'dʌktə(r)/
connection n /kə'nekʃn/
consider v /kən'sɪdə(r)/
continue v /kən'tɪnju:/
county n /'kaunti/
couple n /'kʌpl/
court n /kɔ:t/
creator n /kri'eɪtə(r)/
Dame Commander of the Order
    of the British Empire n /,deɪm
    kə,mɑ:ndər əv ði ,ɔ:dər əv ðə
    ,brɪtɪʃ 'empaɪə(r)/
Dame of the British Empire n
    /,deɪm əv ðə ,brɪtɪʃ
    'empaɪə(r)/

decade n /'dekeɪd/
degree n /dɪ'gri:/
democratically adv
    /,demə'krætɪkli/
design v /dɪ'zaɪn/
detection n /dɪ'tekʃn/
detective n /dɪ'tektɪv/
direct adj, v /də'rekt, dɪ-, daɪ-/
director n /də'rektə(r), dɪ-, daɪ-/
disadvantaged adj
    /,dɪsəd'vɑ:ntɪdʒd/
discovery n /dɪ'skʌvəri/
distinctive adj /dɪ'stɪŋktɪv/
dramatist n /'dræmətɪst/
edition n /ɪ'dɪʃn/
educate v /'edʒukeɪt/
efficient adj /ɪ'fɪʃnt/
Egypt n /'i:dʒɪpt/
Egyptian adj /ɪ'dʒɪpʃn/
elect v /ɪ'lekt/
empty v /'empti/
encyclopaedia n /ɪn,saɪklə'pi:diə/
ending n /'endɪŋ/
especially adv /ɪ'speʃli/
export n /'ekspɔ:t/
extracts n pl /'ekstrækts/
fight against v /'faɪt ə,genst/
final n /'faɪnl/
folio n /'fəuliəu/
footballers n pl /'futbɔ:ləz/
foreign adj /'fɒrən/
funeral n /'fju:nərəl/
goals n pl /gəulz/
grammar school n /'græmə
    ,sku:l/
hero n /'hɪərəu/
ill-documented adj /'ɪl
    ,dɒkjəmentɪd/
Imam n /ɪ'mɑ:m/
importance n /ɪm'pɔ:təns/
imprison v /ɪm'prɪzn/
incorrect adj /,ɪnkə'rekt/
initially adv /ɪ'nɪʃəli/
international adj /,ɪntə'næʃnəl/
Internet n /'ɪntənet/
Iraq n /ɪ'rɑ:k/
Islam n /'ɪzlɑ:m/
Islamic adj /ɪz'læmɪk/
jazz n /dʒæz/
keywords n pl /'ki:wɜ:dz/
Khedive n /kə'di:v/
landscape n /'lændskeɪp/
law n /lɔ:/
law school n /'lɔ: ,sku:l/
lead actor n /,li:d 'æktə(r)/
life-cycle n /'laɪf ,saɪkl/
life-story n /'laɪf ,stɔ:ri/
literary adj /'lɪtərəri/
literature n /'lɪtrətʃə(r)/
luxurious adj /'lʌgʒuəriəs/
maximum adv /'mæksɪməm/
mercury n /'mɜ:kjəri/
middle class adj /,mɪdl 'klɑ:s/
monthly adj /'mʌnθli/
mourners n pl /'mɔ:nəz/
movement n /'mu:vmənt/

movie n /'mu:vi/
mystery n /'mɪstri/
mysterious adj /mɪs'tɪəriəs/
name v /neɪm/
Nobel Prize n /,nəubel 'praɪz/
non-defining relative clause n /
    ,nɒn dɪ,faɪnɪŋ ,relətɪv 'klɔ:z/
noted adj /'nəutɪd/
novel n /'nɒvl/
novelist n /'nɒvəlɪst/
obtain v /əb'teɪn/
omit v /ə'mɪt/
online adj /'ɒnlaɪn/
of all time adv /əv ,ɔ:l 'taɪm/
opera n /'ɒpərə/
orchestra n /'ɔ:kɪstrə/
palace n /'pæləs/
peace n /pi:s/
percentage n /pə'sentɪdʒ/
philosopher n /fɪ'lɒsəfə(r)/
playwright n /'pleɪraɪt/
poetic adj /pəu'etɪk/
Poet Laureate n /,pəuɪt 'lɒriət/
poetry n /'pəuətri/
politician n /,pɒlə'tɪʃn/
portrait n /'pɔ:treɪt/
president n /'prezɪdənt/
prison n /'prɪzn/
produce v /prə'dju:s/
prolific adj /prə'lɪfɪk/
prominent adj /'prɒmɪnənt/
prophet n /'prɒfɪt/
prose n /prəuz/
publicly adv /'pʌblɪkli/
publish v /'pʌblɪʃ/
radium n /'reɪdiəm/
rainfall n /'reɪnfɔ:l/
raise v /reɪz/
related to adj /rɪ'leɪtɪd ,tu:, tə/
relative clause n /,relətɪv 'klɔ:z/
relative pronouns n pl /,relətɪv
    'prəunaunz/
release v /rɪ'li:s/
relevant adj /'reləvənt/
reliable adj /rɪ'laɪəbl/
remain v /rɪ'meɪn/
reputation n /,repju'teɪʃn/
retired adj /rɪ'taɪəd/
role n /rəul/
royal adj /'rɔɪəl/
rush v /rʌʃ/
sadly adv /'sædli/
score v /skɔ:(r)/
sculpture n /'skʌlptʃə(r)/
search n /sɜ:tʃ/
search engine n /'sɜ:tʃ ,endʒɪn/
selected adj /sɪ'lektɪd/
separation n /,sepə'reɪʃn/
share v /ʃeə(r)/
short story n /,ʃɔ:t 'stɔ:ri/
sites n pl /saɪts/
songwriter n /'sɒŋraɪtə(r)/
source n /sɔ:s/
South Africa n /,sauθ 'æfrɪkə/
special effects n pl /,speʃl ɪ'fekts/
stages n pl /'steɪdʒɪz/
star n, v /stɑ:(r)/

statesman *n* /'steɪtsmən/
subject *n* /'sʌbdʒɪkt/
surprising *adj* /sə'praɪzɪŋ/
Switzerland *n* /'swɪtsələnd/
Syria *n* /'sɪriə/
teens *n pl* /ti:nz/
topic *n* /'tɒpɪk/
tournament *n* /'tɔ:nəmənt/
tragedy *n* /'trædʒədi/
tragicomedy *n* /,trædʒɪ'kɒmədi/
tribute *n* /'trɪbju:t/
trip *n* /trɪp/
unhappy *adj* /ʌn'hæpi/
Unicef *n* /'ju:nɪsef/
unique *adj* /ju:'ni:k/
unknown *adj* /ʌn'nəʊn/
volumes *n pl* /'vɒlju:mz/
website *n* /'websaɪt/
well-connected *adj* /,wel
    kə'nektɪd/
widely-read *adj* /,waɪdli 'red/
works *n pl* /wɜ:ks/
World Cup *n* /,wɜ:ld 'kʌp/
Zimbabwe *n* /zɪm'ba:bwi/

Unit 8

abbreviations *n pl* /ə,bri:vi'eɪʃnz/
access *v* /'ækses/
accurate *adj* /'ækjərət/
acknowledge *v* /ək'nɒlɪdʒ/
acknowledgements *n pl*
    /ək'nɒlɪdʒmənts/
acronyms *n pl* /'ækrənɪmz/
advertising *n* /'ædvətaɪzɪŋ/
aerial *n* /'eərial/
afford *v* /ə'fɔ:d/
alphabetical *adj* /,ælfə'betɪkl/
anti-spam *adj* /,ænti 'spæm/
anti-virus *adj* /,ænti 'vaɪrəs/
as *conj* /əz/
as a result *adv* /,əz ə rɪ'zʌlt/
attack *n, v* /ə'tæk/
attractive *adj* /ə'træktɪv/
backup *v* /'bækʌp, ,bæk 'ʌp/
basic *adj* /'beɪsɪk/
batteries *n pl* /'bætəriz/
BBC *n* /,bi: bi: 'si:/
be made up of *v* /,bɪ 'meɪd ʌp
    əv/
bibliography *n* /,bɪbli'ɒgrəfi/
biochemistry *n* /,baɪəʊ'kemɪstri/
brackets *n pl* /'brækɪts/
brain *n* /breɪn/
break into *v* /'breɪk ,ɪntə/
breakthrough *n* /'breɪkθru:/
c. / ca. /'sɜ:kə/
CD burner *n* /,si: 'dɜ: ,bɜ:nə(r)/
CD-ROM *n* /,si: di: 'rɒm/
central processing unit *n* /,sentrəl
    'prəʊsesɪŋ ,ju:nɪt/
certainly *adv* /'sɜ:tnli/
cf. /'si: ef/
chips (computer chips) *n pl*
    /tʃɪps/
circa *prep* /'sɜ:kə/

codes *n pl* /kəʊdz/
coherent *adj* /kəʊ'hɪərənt/
cohesive *adj* /kəʊ'hi:sɪv/
commercial *adj* /kə'mɜ:ʃl/
companies *n pl* /'kʌmpəniz/
connect *v* /kə'nekt/
consequently *adv* /'kɒnsɪkwəntli/
CPU *n* /,si: pi: 'ju:/
crash *v* /kræʃ/
credit *v* /'kredɪt/
credit card *n* /'kredɪt ,ka:d/
crime *n* /kraɪm/
dentist *n* /'dentɪst/
dentistry *n* /'dentɪstri/
department *n* /dɪ'pa:tmənt/
design *n* /dɪ'zaɪn/
designers *n pl* /dɪ'zaɪnəz/
destroy *v* /dɪ'strɔɪ/
details *n pl* /'di:teɪlz/
detect *v* /dɪ'tekt/
developing world *n* /dɪ,veləpɪŋ
    'wɜ:ld/
device *n* /dɪ'vaɪs/
devise *v* /dɪ'vaɪz/
digital *adj* /'dɪdʒɪtl/
download *v* /,daʊn'ləʊd/
drills *n pl* /drɪlz/
DVD burner *n* /,di: vi: 'di:
    ,bɜ:nə(r)/
effectively *adv* /ɪ'fektɪvli/
e.g. /'i: dʒi:/
electricity *n* /ɪ,lek'trɪsəti/
employees *n pl* /,ɪmplɔɪ'i:z/
enormously *adv* /ɪ'nɔ:məsli/
equal *v* /'i:kwəl/
etc. /et'setərə/
for instance /fər 'ɪnstəns/
function *n* /'fʌŋkʃn/
gangs *n pl* /gæŋz/
GB (gigabyte) *n* /gɪg, 'gɪgəbaɪt/
generation *n* /,dʒenə'reɪʃn/
graduates *n pl* /'grædjʊəts/
handle *n* /'hændl/
hardware *n* /'ha:dweə(r)/
hire *v* /haɪə(r)/
house *v* /haʊz/
ibid. /'ɪbɪd/
i.e. /'aɪ i:/
imply *v* /ɪm'plaɪ/
incoming call *n* /,ɪnkʌmɪŋ 'kɔ:l/
individual *adj* /,ɪndɪ'vɪdʒuəl/
information technology *n*
    /,ɪnfə,meɪʃn tek'nɒlədʒi/
in full *adv* /,ɪn 'fʊl/
initial *n* /ɪ'nɪʃl/
in other words /,ɪn 'ʌðə ,wɜ:dz/
install *v* /ɪn'stɔ:l/
Internet *n* /'ɪntənet/
in theory /,ɪn 'θɪəri/
inventions *n pl* /ɪn'venʃnz/
inverted commas *n pl* /ɪn,vɜ:tɪd
    'kɒməz/
iPod *n* /'aɪpɒd/
IT *n* /,aɪ 'ti:/
junk mail *n* /'dʒʌŋk ,meɪl/
keyboard *n* /'ki:bɔ:d/

laptop (computer) *n* /'læptɒp/
laser *n* /'leɪzə(r)/
linking words *n pl* /'lɪŋkɪŋ ,wɜ:dz/
load *v* /ləʊd/
machinery *n* /mə'ʃi:nəri/
mail *n* /meɪl/
mailboxes *n pl* /'meɪlbɒksɪz/
manufacturers *n pl*
    /,mænjə'fæktʃərəz/
memory *n* /'meməri/
memory key *n* /'meməri ,ki:/
monitor *n* /'mɒnɪtə(r)/
mouse *n* /maʊs/
N.B. /,en 'bi:/
networks *n pl* /'netwɜ:ks/
online *adv* /,ɒn 'laɪn/
OPEC *n* /'əʊpek/
opportunity *n* /,ɒpə'tju:nəti/
options *n pl* /'ɒpʃnz/
ordinary *adj* /'ɔ:dnri/
out of control *adj* /,aʊt əv
    kən'trəʊl/
p. / pp. /'pi:, 'pi: pi:/
painless *adj* /'peɪnləs/
password *n* /'pa:swɜ:d/
periodic table *n* /'pɪəriɒdɪk ,teɪbl/
personalize *v* /'pɜ:sənəlaɪz/
personal stereo *n* /,pɜ:sənl
    'steriəʊ/
pharmaceutical *adj*
    /,fa:mə'sju:tɪkl/
phishing *n* /'fɪʃɪŋ/
plug in *v* /,plʌg 'ɪn/
podcasts *n pl* /'pɒdka:sts/
power *v* /'paʊə(r)/
powerful *adj* /'paʊəfl/
printer *n* /'prɪntə(r)/
processing *n* /'prəʊsesɪŋ/
program *n* /'prəʊgræm/
programming *n* /'prəʊgræmɪŋ/
publication *n* /,pʌblɪ'keɪʃn/
publisher *n* /'pʌblɪʃə(r)/
RAM *n* /ræm/
receiver *n* /rɪ'si:və(r)/
recommend *v* /,rekə'mend/
reference *n* /'refrəns/
research *n* /rɪ'sɜ:tʃ, 'ri:sɜ:tʃ/
R/W *n* /,ri:'raɪtə(r), ,ri:'raɪtəbl/
repetition *n* /,repə'tɪʃn/
rephrase *v* /,ri:'freɪz/
scanner *n* /'skænə(r)/
screen *n* /skri:n/
since *conj* /sɪns/
sockets *n pl* /'sɒkɪts/
software *n* /'sɒftweə(r)/
solar energy *n* /,səʊlər 'enədʒi/
sophisticated *adj* /sə'fɪstɪkeɪtɪd/
spam *n* /spæm/
speakers *n pl* /'spi:kəz/
spyware *n* /'spaɪweə(r)/
stand-alone *adj* /'stænd ə,ləʊn/
stand for *v* /'stænd ,fɔ:(r), fə(r)/
storage *n* /'stɔ:rɪdʒ/
strength *n* /streŋθ/
supply *n* /sə'plaɪ/
surname *n* /'sɜ:neɪm/
switch *v* /swɪtʃ/

system *n* /'sɪstəm/
technical *adj* /'teknɪkl/
text message *n* /'tekst ,mesɪdʒ/
that is /'ðæt ɪz/
that is to say /'ðæt ɪz tə ,seɪ/
threat *n* /θret/
training *n* /'treɪnɪŋ/
treatment *n* /'tri:tmənt/
trick *v, n* /trɪk/
Trojan Horse *n* /,trəʊdʒən 'hɔ:s/
UK *n* /,ju: 'keɪ/
unit *n* /'ju:nɪt/
uncertain *adj* /ʌn'sɜ:tn/
unwanted *adj* /ʌn'wɒntɪd/
up-to-date *adj* /,ʌp tə 'deɪt/
USB port *n* /,ju: es 'bi: ,pɔ:t/
user ID *n* /,ju:zər ,aɪ 'di:/
VDU *n* /,vi: di: 'ju:/
via *prep* /'vaɪə/
vibrate *v* /vaɪ'breɪt/
virus *n* /'vaɪrəs/
webcam *n* /'webkæm/
webpage *n* /'webpeɪdʒ/
WiFi *n* /'waɪfaɪ/
wind up *adj* /'waɪnd ʌp/
wireless *n* /'waɪələs/
www /,dʌbl ju: ,dʌbl ju: 'dʌbl
    ju:/

Unit 9

add *v* /æd/
aerial *n* /'eərial/
after that *adv* /,a:ftə 'ðæt/
alkali *n* /'ælkəlaɪ/
amplifier *n* /'æmplɪfaɪə(r)/
answerphone *n* /'a:nsəfəʊn/
appropriately *adv* /ə'prəʊpriətli/
atmosphere *n* /'ætməsfɪə(r)/
benefits *n pl* /'benəfɪts/
biochemist *n* /,baɪəʊ'kemɪst/
blue-eyed *adj* /,blu: 'aɪd/
carrier waves *n pl* /'kæriə ,weɪvz/
category *n* /'kætəgəri/
communication *n*
    /kə,mju:nɪ'keɪʃn/
compound noun *n* /,kɒmpaʊnd
    'naʊn/
compress *v* /kəm'pres/
computer literate *adj* /kəm,pju:tə
    'lɪtərət/
cordless phone *n* /,kɔ:dləs 'fəʊn/
data-processing *n* /,deɪtə
    'prəʊsesɪŋ/
deoxyribose nucleic acid *n*
    /di,ɒksi,raɪbəʊz ,nju:kli:ɪk
    'æsɪd/
detailed *adj* /'di:teɪld/
diesel engine *n* /'di:zl ,endʒɪn/
dinosaurs *n pl* /'daɪnəsɔ:z/
discovery *n* /dɪ'skʌvəri/
distil *v* /dɪ'stɪl/
dodos *n pl* /'dəʊdəʊz/
Dominica *n* /,dɒmɪ'ni:kə/
dove *n* /dʌv/
dragon *n* /'drægən/

drum *n* /drʌm/
dry *v* /draɪ/
dynamite *n* /'daɪnəmaɪt/

easy-going *adj* /,i:zi 'gəʊɪŋ/
eclipses *n pl* /ɪ'klɪpsɪz/
ecology *n* /ɪ'kɔlədʒi/
Ecuador *n* /'ekwədɔ:(r)/
electronic *adj* /ɪ,lek'trɒnɪk/
engine *n* /'endʒɪn/
entertainment *n* /,entə'teɪnmənt/
expand *v* /ɪk'spænd/
experiments *n pl* /ɪk'sperɪmənts/
extinct *adj* /ɪk'stɪŋkt/

fax machine *n* /'fæks mə,ʃi:n/
firstly *adv* /'fɜ:stli/
flight *n* /flaɪt/
focused *adj* /'fəʊkəst/
freely *adv* /'fri:li/
furnace *n* /'fɜ:nɪs/

hard-working *adj* /,hɑ:d 'wɜ:kɪŋ/
headphones *n pl* /'hedfəʊnz/
highly-qualified *adj* /,haɪli 'kwɒlɪfaɪd/
high-speed *adj* /'haɪ ,spi:d/
index *n* /'ɪndeks/
infrastructure *n* /'ɪnfrə,strʌktʃə(r)/
internal combustion engine *n* / ɪn,tɜ:nl kəm'bʌstʃən ,endʒɪn/
interviewers *n pl* /'ɪntəvju:əz/
invent *v* /ɪn'vent/
invention *n* /ɪn'venʃn/
invisible *adj* /ɪn'vɪzəbl/

lastly *adv* /'lɑ:stli/
light bulbs *n pl* /'laɪt ,bʌlbz/
limestone *n* /'laɪmstəʊn/
long-term *adj* /,lɒŋ 'tɜ:m/

means *n* /mi:nz/
melt *v* /melt/
microwave oven *n* /,maɪkrəweɪv 'ʌvn/
mix *v* /mɪks/
mixture *n* /'mɪkstʃə(r)/
network *n* /'netwɜ:k/
neutral *adj* /'nju:trəl/
observer *n* /əb'zɜ:və(r)/
overview *n* /'əʊvəvju:/

pack *v* /pæk/
passive *n* /'pæsɪv/
pass through *v* /,pɑ:s 'θru:/
penicillin *n* /,penɪ'sɪlɪn/
perfume *n* /'pɜ:fju:m/
phone line *n* /'fəʊn ,laɪn/
physics laboratory *n* /'fɪzɪks lə,bɒrətri/
pick up *v* /,pɪk 'ʌp/
plug into *v* /'plʌg ,ɪntə/
poorly-written *adj* /,pɔ:li 'rɪtn/
press *v* /pres/
process *n* /'prəʊses/
professor *n* /prə'fesə(r)/

quality *n* /'kwɒləti/

radio waves *n pl* /'reɪdiəʊ ,weɪvz/
receiving aerial *n* /rɪ'si:vɪŋ ,eəriəl/

recycle *v* /,ri:'saɪkl/
reference book *n* /'refrəns ,bʊk/
remote control *n* /rɪ,məʊt kən'trəʊl/
remote-controlled *adj* /rɪ'məʊt kən,trəʊld/
reverse process *n* /rɪ'vɜ:s ,prəʊses/
roll *v* /rəʊl/

sand *n* /sænd/
satellite dish *n* /'sætəlaɪt ,dɪʃ/
secondly *adv* /'sekəndli/
self-motivated *adj* /,self 'məʊtɪveɪtɪd/
send out *v* /,send 'aʊt/
sequencing words *n pl* / 'si:kwənsɪŋ ,wɜ:dz/
side-effects *n pl* /'saɪd ɪ,fekts/
signals *n pl* /'sɪgnəlz/
silica *n* /'sɪlɪkə/
simple *adj* /'sɪmpl/
small-scale *adj* /'smɔ:l ,skeɪl/
soda ash *n* /'səʊdər ,æʃ/
speakers *n pl* /'spi:kəz/
steam engine *n* /'sti:m ,endʒɪn/
step *n* /step/
studio *n* /'stju:diəʊ/
subsequently *adv* /'sʌbsɪkwəntli/

tables *n pl* /'teɪblz/
total *adj* /'təʊtl/
transistor radio *n* /træn,zɪstə 'reɪdiəʊ/
turn back into *v* /'tɜ:n ,bæk ,ɪntə/

undetectable *adj* /,ʌndɪ'tektəbl/

voice-powered *adj* /'vɔɪs ,paʊəd/
voice waves *n pl* /'vɔɪs ,weɪvz/

waves *n pl* /weɪvz/
well-known *adj* /,wel 'nəʊn/
well-written *adj* /,wel 'rɪtn/
widespread *adj* /'waɪdspred/
wireless *adj* /'waɪələs/
word processor *n* /,wɜ:d 'prəʊsesə(r)/
wrap *v* /ræp/

X-rays *n pl* /'eks ,reɪz/

Unit 10

academic *adj* /,ækə'demɪk/
apart from *prep* /ə'pɑ:t frəm/
appropriate *adj* /ə'prəʊpriət/
approximately *adv* /ə'prɒksɪmətli/
Arabic *n* /'ærəbɪk/

bar chart *n* /'bɑ: ,tʃɑ:t/
Bengali *n* /beŋ'gɔ:li/

charts *n pl* /tʃɑ:ts/
China *n* /'tʃaɪnə/
comparatives *n pl* /kəm'pærətɪvz/
comparison *n* /kəm'pærɪsn/
continual *adj* /kən'tɪnjʊəl/

decrease *n, v* /'di:kri:s, dɪ'kri:s/
destinations *n pl* /,destɪ'neɪʃnz/
diagram *n* /'daɪəgræm/
dramatic *adj* /drə'mætɪk/
dramatically *adv* /drə'mætɪkli/

drop *n, v* /drɒp/
fall *n, v* /fɔ:l/
fluctuate *v* /'flʌktʃueɪt/
foreign *adj* /'fɒrən/
France *n* /frɑ:ns/
French *adj* /frentʃ/

graph *n* /grɑ:f/
grow *v* /grəʊ/
growth *n* /grəʊθ/

Hindi *n* /'hɪndi/
horizontal *adj* /,hɒrɪ'zɒntl/
Hungary *n* /'hʌŋgəri/

illustrate *v* /'ɪləstreɪt/
increase *n, v* /'ɪŋkri:s, ɪn'kri:s/
interpret *v* /ɪn'tɜ:prɪt/

Japan *n* /dʒə'pæn/
Japanese *adj* /,dʒæpə'ni:z/

lowest point *n* /'ləʊɪst ,pɔɪnt/

Mandarin Chinese *n* /,mændərɪn tʃaɪ'ni:z/
Mexico *n* /'meksɪkəʊ/

overall *adj* /,əʊvər'ɔ:l/

peak *n* /pi:k/
percentage *n* /pə'sentɪdʒ/
period *n* /'pɪəriəd/
Poland *n* /'pəʊlənd/
Portuguese *n* /,pɔ:tʃʊ'gi:z/

refer to *v* /rɪ'fɜ: ,tu:, tə/
remain *v* /rɪ'meɪn/
require *v* /rɪ'kwaɪə(r)/
respectively *adv* /rɪ'spektɪvli/
rise *n, v* /raɪz/
Russia *n* /'rʌʃə/
Russian *adj, n* /'rʌʃn/

scientific *adj* /,saɪən'tɪfɪk/
significantly *adv* /sɪg'nɪfɪkəntli/
slight *adj* /slaɪt/
slightly *adv* /slaɪtli/
Spain *n* /speɪn/
Spanish *n* /'spænɪʃ/
spot *n* /spɒt/
stable *adj* /'steɪbl/
statistical *adj* /stə'tɪstɪkl/
statistics *n pl* /stə'tɪstɪks/
steadily *adv* /'stedəli/
steady *adj* /'stedi/
sudden *adj* /'sʌdn/
suddenly *adv* /'sʌdnli/
superlatives *n pl* /su:'pɜ:lətɪvz/

trend *n* /trend/

unexpected *adj* /,ʌnɪk'spektɪd/
USA *n* /,ju: es 'eɪ/

vary *v* /'veəri/
vertical *adj* /'vɜ:tɪkl/
whereas *conj* /,weər'æz/

Phonetic symbols

Consonants

1	/p/	as in	**pen** /pen/
2	/b/	as in	**big** /bɪg/
3	/t/	as in	**tea** /tiː/
4	/d/	as in	**do** /duː/
5	/k/	as in	**cat** /kæt/
6	/g/	as in	**go** /gəʊ/
7	/f/	as in	**four** /fɔː/
8	/v/	as in	**very** /'veri/
9	/s/	as in	**son** /sʌn/
10	/z/	as in	**zoo** /zuː/
11	/l/	as in	**live** /lɪv/
12	/m/	as in	**my** /maɪ/
13	/n/	as in	**near** /nɪə/
14	/h/	as in	**happy** /'hæpi/
15	/r/	as in	**red** /red/
16	/j/	as in	**yes** /jes/
17	/w/	as in	**want** /wɒnt/
18	/θ/	as in	**thanks** /θæŋks/
19	/ð/	as in	**the** /ðə/
20	/ʃ/	as in	**she** /ʃiː/
21	/ʒ/	as in	**television** /'telɪvɪʒn/
22	/tʃ/	as in	**child** /tʃaɪld/
23	/dʒ/	as in	**German** /'dʒɜːmən/
24	/ŋ/	as in	**English** /'ɪŋglɪʃ/

Vowels

25	/iː/	as in	**see** /siː/
26	/ɪ/	as in	**his** /hɪz/
27	/i/	as in	**twenty** /'twenti/
28	/e/	as in	**ten** /ten/
29	/æ/	as in	**stamp** /stæmp/
30	/ɑː/	as in	**father** /'fɑːðə/
31	/ɒ/	as in	**hot** /hɒt/
32	/ɔː/	as in	**morning** /'mɔːnɪŋ/
33	/ʊ/	as in	**football** /'fʊtbɔːl/
34	/uː/	as in	**you** /juː/
35	/ʌ/	as in	**sun** /sʌn/
36	/ɜː/	as in	**learn** /lɜːn/
37	/ə/	as in	**letter** /'letə/

Diphthongs (two vowels together)

38	/eɪ/	as in	**name** /neɪm/
39	/əʊ/	as in	**no** /nəʊ/
40	/aɪ/	as in	**my** /maɪ/
41	/aʊ/	as in	**how** /haʊ/
42	/ɔɪ/	as in	**boy** /bɔɪ/
43	/ɪə/	as in	**hear** /hɪə/
44	/eə/	as in	**where** /weə/
45	/ʊə/	as in	**tour** /tʊə/

OXFORD
UNIVERSITY PRESS

Great Clarendon Street, Oxford, OX2 6DP, United Kingdom

Oxford University Press is a department of the University of Oxford.
It furthers the University's objective of excellence in research, scholarship,
and education by publishing worldwide. Oxford is a registered trade
mark of Oxford University Press in the UK and in certain other countries

© Oxford University Press 2011

The moral rights of the author have been asserted

First published in 2011

2016 2015 2014 2013

10 9 8 7 6

ISBN: 978 0 19 474160 6

Printed in China

This book is printed on paper from certified and well-managed sources

ACKNOWLEDGEMENTS

Illustrations by: Peter Bull, p.40; Mark Duffin, pp.14, 26, 53, 62; Gavin Reece,
p.21, 46

Commissioned photography by: Pearl Bevan, p.6

*We would also like to thank the following for permission to reproduce the following
photographs*: Alamy pp.7 (Glow Image), 11 (Singapore/Chad Ehlers), (Morocco/
JTB Photo), (Wales/John Henshall), 13 (Everest/MaryEllen McGrath/Bruce
Coleman Inc.), (Sydney/Andrew Morse), 16 (hotel/Helene Rogers), 24 (D. Hurst),
25 (Andrew Linscott), 27 (plane/Image Source), 29 (Peter Adams Photography),
37 (bilderlounge media GmbH/Claudia Göpperl), 42 Stock Connection
Distribution/Dean Lipoff; 51a (phone/Simon Hadley), 52 (Mary Evans Picture
Library), 54 (doug steley), 55 (microwave/Stockdisc Classic), (telephone/
Stockbyte Silver), (television/V&A Images); Auto Express Picture Library
p.23 (car); Courtesy of The Cambridge-MIT Institute (CMI) p.23 (plane); Corbis
pp.15 (Tom Van Sant), 19 (man with beard/Royalty-Free/Corbis), (man with hat/
Jed & Kaoru Share), 27 (watch/Reuters/Fabrizio Bensch), 40 (Shakespeare/
Bettmann), 43 (Zidane/Christian Liewig), (Federer/Rhona Wise/epa), 45 (Jean-
Philippe Arles/Reuters), 48 (MIT Media Lab/epa), 55 (flight/Underwood &
Underwood), (steam engine/Philip Gendreau); 58a (Paul Hardy); 58b (Sylvain
Sonnet); Empics p.44 (Mandela older/Mok Yui Mok/PA); Getty Images
pp.4 (Photosindia), 12 (John Lawrence), 13 (Sahara/Daniele Pellegrini), (Nile/
Sylvain Grandadam), 16 (Frank/Siri Stafford), (plane baggage hold/Siri
Stafford), 19 (chauffeur/Rob Melnychuk), 31 (Stockbyte), 33 (Dr Kuffash/
Photonica), 35 (Taxi), 39 (food/Michael Rosenfeld), 43 (Curie/Hulton Archive/
Stringer), 55 (wheel/Dorling Kindersley), 58 (Hungary/Photographer's Choice/
Hiroshi Higuchi), (China/The Image Bank/Gavin Hellier), (Canada/
Photographer's Choice/Jacob Taposchaner); Geoff Holdsworth p.51 (Freeview
box); Photolibrary.com p.39 (foot/BSIP); Rex Features pp.36 (Action Press),
40 (Christie/Everett Collection), 51 (dentist drill/Voisin/Phanie), 55 (internal
combustion engine/Mimmo Frassineti); Science Photo Library
p.39 (tuberculosis/Alfred Pasieka); Still Pictures p.34 (Ulstein/Oberhaeuser);
Science & Society Picture Library p.55 (computer/Science Museum)

*The authors and publisher are grateful to those who have given permission to reproduce
the following extracts and adaptations of copyright material*: p.8 entries from the
Oxford Student's Dictionary of English © Oxford University Press 2001. Reproduced
by kind permission. p.30 extract from *Regeneration* by Pat Barker (Viking 1992)
© Pat Barker 1992. Reproduced by permission of Penguin Group (UK). p.30
extract from *Lecture Notes on Clinical Medicine* by David Rubenstein. Reproduced
by kind permission of Blackwell Publishing. p.30 adapted extract from *The
Medieval Economy and Society* by M.M. Postan (Pelican, 1975) © M.M. Postan 1975.
Reproduced by kind permission of Penguin Group (UK). p.26 entries from the
Oxford Student's Dictionary of English © Oxford University Press 2001. Reproduced
by kind permission.

Sources: p.59 http://geography.about.com/library/weekly/aa050899.htmp.35
The Scientific American, 21 September 2005

*Although every effort has been made to trace and contact copyright holders before
publication, this has not been possible in some cases. We apologise for any apparent
infringement of copyright and, if notified, the publisher will be pleased to rectify any
errors or omissions at the earliest possible opportunity.*